BEYOND
BOOK
ONE

BEYOND BOOK ONE

HOW TO PLAN AND PUBLISH A SUCCESSFUL FICTIONAL SERIES

LEWIS JORSTAD

THE NOVEL SMITHY

Beyond Book One: How to Plan and Publish a Successful Fictional Series

Copyright © 2023 Lewis Jorstad

The Writer's Craft Series — Book Three

Published by The Novel Smithy, LLC.

Printed in the United States of America.

1st Edition, 2023

ISBN (print): 978-1-955157-09-4

ISBN (digital): 978-1-955157-10-0

ISBN (hardcover): 978-1-955157-11-7

https://thenovelsmithy.com/

❦ Created with Vellum

ALSO BY LEWIS JORSTAD

THE TEN DAY NOVELIST SERIES

The Ten Day Outline
The Ten Day Draft
The Ten Day Edit
The Ten Day Author

———

THE WRITER'S CRAFT SERIES

Write Your Hero
Mastering Character Arcs
Beyond Book One

CONTENTS

Before you go... **How well do you really know your hero?**

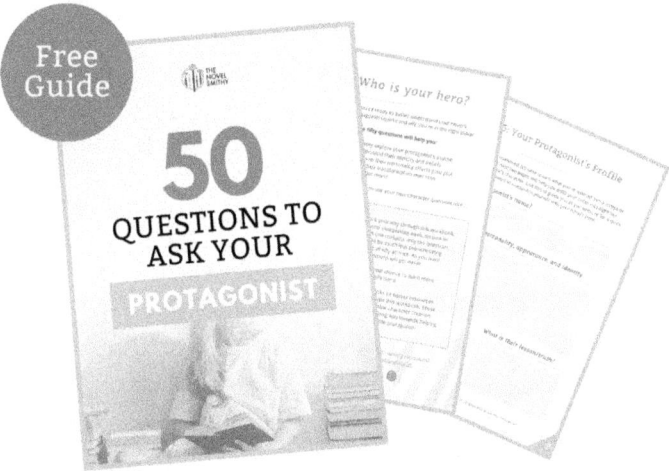

If you're ready to craft a vibrant, engaging protagonist, download your **FREE copy of 50 Questions to Ask Your Protagonist.**

This in-depth questionnaire is the perfect companion to this book, and the perfect way to get to know your hero!

https://thenovelsmithy.com/50-questions/

INTRODUCTION
IT'S ALL IN THE NAME

"So, how *do* you write a series worth reading?"

This was the question that first sparked this book, and that slowly spiraled into more and more research as *Beyond Book One* took shape. Why are some series so different from others? Why are there so few terms to describe fictional series? What about trilogies, extended universes, and prequels? And how do you turn a standalone novel into a series without stretching the story to the point of breaking?

Those were the questions on my mind when I started digging into this topic years ago, and they soon revealed a whole world of series structure I never knew existed. So many writing resources are geared towards standalone novels first and foremost—but series turn nearly all of those structures on their head.

Your characters won't look the same in a twelve-book spy thriller as they do in a short duology.

Your plot will unfold differently in an urban fantasy trilogy compared to a long-running romance.

Even the simple matter of writing a sequel adds an entirely new set of obstacles for you to face.

Series really are their own animal, with challenges, joys, and nuances all in equal measure. And they're not going away anytime soon! Not only can a series be tremendously fun to write (even if it's a lot to manage), but well-written series are the true backbone of so many author careers.

That's where this book comes in.

Beyond Book One aims to fill the gap between traditional storytelling tools and the world of successful fictional series. Over the next fourteen chapters, we'll take the writing skills you've already built (or may build in the future) and help you apply them to a connected *string* of novels—rather than just a standalone.

You'll learn:

- The four fundamental patterns that underpin successful fictional series
- How to craft powerful series plots and characters that keep readers hooked
- The three-part rhythm unique to writing a trilogy
- Ways to avoid burnout, write riveting prequels, and more
- And how to create a book launch plan to help you publish your new series

Whether you end this book with a ten-part sci-fi epic rattling around in your brain, or land on a short and sweet romance duology, I hope this becomes a reliable guide as you set out on your own series-writing adventures!

NOTE: This book is part of a larger series on the craft of writing. However, you don't need to have read those books to enjoy this one. While I certainly recommend those guides, all you need to start *Beyond Book One* is an idea for your story and a spare afternoon!

I

FOUR SIMPLE
STRUCTURES

"The pages are still blank, but there is a miraculous feeling of the words being there, written in invisible ink and clamoring to become visible."

VLADIMIR NABOKOV

1

A PUBLISHING POWERHOUSE

S eries are a lot like works of art—you know one when you see it.

However, that disguises the real complexity of good fictional series. *The Lord of the Rings* is a fantasy series, but so are *Redwall*, *The Graceling Realm*, and *The Earthsea Cycle*. And if you know much about those books, you'll know that they're vastly different, despite sharing the "series" moniker. Same with *Nancy Drew* and *The Sevenwaters Trilogy*, *Jack Reacher* and the *Dune Chronicles*...

Even if your novels are connected by nothing more than the picturesque beach town they take place in, they can still work as a series if you know what you're doing!

That premise is the real core of this book, and the first thing we'll be focusing on throughout Part One. We have a lot to explore during our time together—but before we talk publishing tricks or writing styles, you need to know what type of series you're setting out to write in the first place.

Why Write a Series?

Though series can be hard to pin down, they do follow a basic definition. To count as a series, your novels need to be linked by an overarching plot, a common cast of characters, a familiar world, or a shared concept—though not always at the same time. More on that in a moment.

This is what makes series both magical and complicated.

For authors, a series gives you tons of flexibility to explore large casts of characters, expansive conflicts, and complex worldbuilding. If you're bursting at the seams with exciting ideas, writing a series ensures you have plenty of room to enjoy them.

Some stories simply won't fit in eighty thousand words!

This is great for readers as well. If you publish a series consistently, readers get the benefit of regular, bingeable content—and it's a lot easier to jump into a novel when you already know what you're getting into. There's power in familiarity. It's comforting to curl up with a series you love, because you already have a relationship with the characters and world you're about to inhabit. In many ways, it's a lot like visiting an old friend.

All of this adds up to an important truth for authors: Series are often the best path towards financial success.

Don't get me wrong. Plenty of standalone novels do quite well for their authors, and plenty of series don't. Still, there's no denying that most career authors write in long-running series for a reason.

There's a much lower barrier to entry for readers. Those who enjoyed book one will be more apt to continue to book two, versus starting an entirely new story. And because of this, it's a lot easier to build a dedicated fan base on the back of a series. Someone who reads just one standalone novel might not be all that attached to you as an author. But, someone who has read every book in a six-book series probably will be.

Of course, this all hinges on the quality of your series—just because you slap the number two in the name doesn't mean readers will stick around if you don't make it worth their time. There's always a certain level of resistance when readers finish one novel and are about to start the next. If your series doesn't guide them through a meaningful story, it's easy to set it down for good.

Four Types of Successful Series

This brings us to the real difference between standalone novels and series.

While a standalone novel is fully self-contained and thus a complete experience in its own right, a series has to account for every book in the set. This is done on two main levels:

- **The Book-Specific Plot:** The individual plot for each book in the series, similar to a standalone novel. This plot follows all the same rules as any other story, to ensure each novel is satisfying to read even though it's only one part of a larger tale.
- **The Overarching Concept:** The big idea (often in the form of a larger plot, cast, or conflict) that links every book in the series. This stretches from beginning to end, and binds the series together as a cohesive whole.

Now, right away you might be thinking, "I've read plenty of series with no overarching plot to speak of, or even overarching characters." And you'd be right! This is why series are hard to define. While *A Song of Ice and Fire* has the same plot and heroes stretching throughout the series, *The Kiss Quotient* doesn't—and that's ok.

This is because that overarching concept can work in a few ways.

In some series, it's a common conflict or threat, while in others it's the same protagonist, the same world, or the same setup. There's a huge variety here, but no matter what series you pick up, it'll usually fall into one of four categories:

- **Sequential Series:** A series built around a clear, overarching plot, often told through three or more full-length novels. This type of series is the most like a standalone novel in terms of structure (more on that in Chapter Two), and is what many authors traditionally think of as a "series." Common in nearly all genres, but especially fantasy and science fiction.
- **Episodic Series:** A series that mimics TV shows. Episodic series use novellas or short novels to tell a large, overarching plot, but with room for side quests and sub-stories. Though similar to sequential series, episodic series rely on much smaller installments and thus play by slightly different rules.
- **Static Series:** The classic monster-of-the-week series! Static series lack an overarching plot, and instead focus on a common protagonist as they face similar situations and obstacles in different times and places. This style is especially popular for mysteries and thrillers, where each entry focuses on a new crime or threat.

- **Anthology Series:** The most disconnected series type, and the only one that relies purely on a common setup, theme, or world. Anthology series have no overarching plot, and don't feature the same protagonists across each book. This is commonly seen in romance, where the story follows a new couple in each entry.

If you look closely, you should notice some similarities between sequential and episodic series, and static and anthology series. Though each of these four are distinct, sequential and episodic series are both connected by a single plot that stretches across every book. Static and anthology series lack this common plot, and instead rely on other over-arching concepts to bind them together.

All four work as fictional series, but they do so in their own unique ways.

NOTE: While researching this topic, I found there aren't many agreed-upon terms for describing different series. Though some of these names are more common, most are ones I've chosen for the sake of this book. If there's another name you're used to, know that we're likely talking about the same thing! I'll try to call out other names I've seen over the next few chapters.

Lessons from Chapter One

At the end of the day, it's that overarching concept that really makes something a *series*, rather than a random collection of books. Each of these four styles has its own quirks and nuances, but they all play by the same rules, which allow them to work as fictional series:

- The overarching concept is compelling to the reader
- Each novel is engaging and enjoyable in its own right
- Every entry is meaningfully connected to the rest
- And your overarching concept remains consistent and clear from start to finish

Beyond these basics, the type of series you write will affect a lot of things. Each of these styles creates a very different experience for your readers, and they also affect how you approach both the writing and publishing process.

Fortunately, for most authors, this is well worth the work.

Though series are definitely more complicated than stand-alone novels, that complication is their greatest strength. Writing a series opens up a wealth of opportunities—both for your career as an author and for telling unique and satisfying stories.

The key is knowing what type of series you're writing, why you're drawn to that format, and how you'll handle the practical act of writing it. This is what we'll be building throughout this book, so that by the end, you should have a clear picture of what your series will become.

In the meantime, here are a few questions to help you apply what you've learned to your story:

- What does success look like to you as an author?
- Where does a series fit in your author career?
- What overarching concept could you use to link your series together?

- Which of these four types of series feels most aligned with your vision?

Once you've answered these questions, I'll see you in Chapter Two!

2

SEQUENTIAL VS. EPISODIC

My aunt called me from the door, hoping to coax me away from the TV and out onto the beach.

"Come on, let's go swimming. It's already after lunch!"

Unfortunately for my aunt, I had no interest in going to the beach—or even getting off the couch, for that matter. Though I loved to swim as a kid and was always ecstatic for our annual beach week, this year, I had more important matters to attend to.

The finale of *Avatar: The Last Airbender* was airing, and I wasn't going to miss it for the world.

Now, before you assume I was just being a couch potato, I had been watching this show since the very first season, and this finale was a *huge* deal. The series had been building to this moment since minute one, over sixty episodes ago, and my child hands were gripping the arm of the couch like it was my only lifeline back to the real world. I was hooked, and to this day that finale is still one of the most impactful moments I've ever seen in storytelling, tying the whole series together in ways I never thought possible.

If you were there that summer, you know exactly what I mean!

This right here is the power of a well-written series, whether episodic or sequential. When done right, you've pulled readers into your world and got them to truly love your story. All of this builds to that big moment when your plot comes together, and the payoff is unlike anything else.

Of course, this payoff can also end up epically disappointing, and there are plenty of examples of series that whiffed the landing. A sequential or episodic series involves a lot of moving parts, and you'll need to know what you're getting into if you want to win readers over in those final moments.

That's why, in this chapter, we need to explore these types of series a bit further. There are pitfalls to watch for and quirks to consider, but by the end, you should start to see how you can tie your series together in a way that leaves readers wide-eyed and hearts-racing—just like my childhood self!

The Sequential Series

As we talked about in Chapter One, a sequential series is what many writers think of as the most traditional type of series. These series are classics, taking shape as famous trilogies, powerful YA duologies, six-book sci-fi epics, and more.

A sequential series is built around a clear, overarching plot, told across multiple novels. There's one core cast throughout the series, and each book slowly builds to the grand finale that resolves that main plot. In this way, sequential series are similar to standalone novels, just on a bigger scale. They're telling a single story, but across a handful of installments, each with their own smaller plots that act as building blocks for the whole series.

SEQUENTIAL SERIES STRUCTURE

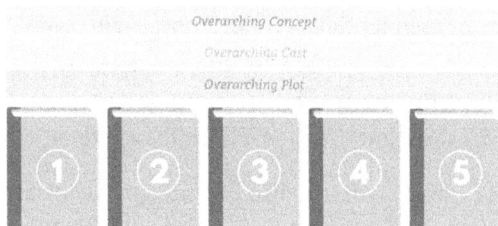

Duologies, trilogies, four-book series, and longer are all common here, but this series type doesn't require a set number of books.

Though trilogies are popular, duologies have been gaining ground in recent years, while longer series are usually found in epic fantasy or science fiction. The *Six of Crows* duology counts as a sequential series just as much as the nearly two-million-word *A Song of Ice and Fire* series. So long as each full-length novel is connected by an overarching plot, you're in business.

That note on "full-length novels" is important, because that's often the fastest way to tell the difference between a sequential and episodic series—though it's not the only difference. We'll chat more about episodic series in a moment, but those series are built around shorter installments, while sequential novels are generally fifty thousand words or longer.

There is still plenty of variety here, though.

Series like *The Lord of the Rings* (where each book is truly one part of an epic story) flow seamlessly from one entry to the next, so much so that I've heard them referred to as continuous series more than once. However, you could also follow in the footsteps of the original *Star Wars* trilogy or *The Hunger Games*. Both of these series feel almost like standalones in their first installment. The conflict is a bit smaller, and it's cleanly wrapped up by the end of that first book. Katniss survives the Games. Luke destroys the Death Star. But, before you can catch your breath, a bigger threat looms —and you realize this was really just the beginning of a much grander tale.

Either way, the best sequential series will fulfill a few things:

- They have a clear core conflict and overarching plot linking each book
- They have a common cast of characters that persist throughout the series
- Each installment moves the story closer to its big finale, where the overarching plot is resolved
- And each book flows naturally to the next, opening a loop (or asking a question) that encourages readers to begin the next phase of the story

The Episodic Series

With sequential series as a baseline, we can shift our focus to their smaller cousin: episodic series.

Episodic series are similar to sequential series, in that they both rely on a single, overarching plot to bind the series together. However, unlike a sequential series, episodic series have more in common with TV shows. These series rely on smaller installments, short stories, and novellas to tell a larger tale, and each "episode" is really just one tiny piece of the larger plot.

This gives episodic series a lot more room to flex.

It's not unusual to have entire episodes dedicated to side quests and subplots, or one-off adventures focused on different characters, relationships, or slice-of-life moments. Many of these episodes won't be strictly tied to the overarching plot, and that's ok. Because episodic series are built on much shorter installments, readers are more willing to stick with you as you explore the various nooks and crannies of your story.

EPISODIC SERIES STRUCTURE

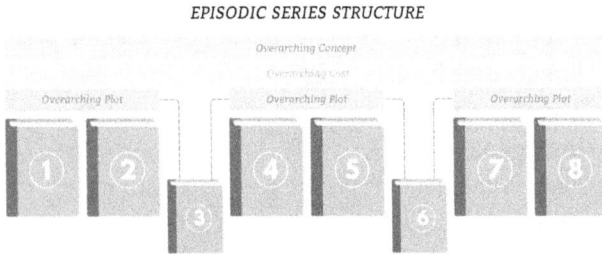

As you can probably imagine, all of this makes episodic series a natural fit for platforms like Kindle Vella, Kindle Unlimited, or Tapas. With these, readers can subscribe to the story, rather than having to buy and wait for each individual entry. This reduces the resistance between books, and makes it easier to jump from episode to episode—whether those are only a few thousand words or entire novellas.

This is where the name "episodic" can get confusing though.

Many of these platforms promote themselves as a place for "serialized fiction," and unsurprisingly, that means readers and writers often use both terms to describe this type of series. However, serials can be a lot of things. Episodic series, short sequential series, and even static series (more on that in the next chapter) can all fall under this name depending on who you talk to. In fact, one of the most famous static series, *Sherlock Holmes*, started life as serialized fiction!

Because of this, I would say that serialized fiction is simply fiction published in small chapters quickly, whether those chapters are truly episodic or not.

What you'll also find with this style of series is that they're often collected into a final "season" after a certain number of books. Again, taking inspiration from TV shows, episodic series often have smaller season arcs that link four, five, or even six books in the series. Though each season is still building towards the larger overarching plot, this helps create strong turning points and an even clearer sense of progress—and it also gives you fun options for how you package and publish your series down the line.

If you're considering this style, keep in mind that the best episodic series fulfill a few things:

- They have a common cast of characters and overarching plot linking each book or season
- They include shorter entries (usually a novella or less) with room for side quests and subplots
- Their faster pace pulls readers from episode to episode, making them inherently bingeable
- And there's generally a consistent length between episodes in the series

Case Study: LOTR vs. Dragon School

To help you see how these types compare, we'll look at two series: *The Lord of the Rings* and Sarah K. L. Wilson's *Dragon School* series.

The Lord of the Rings is one of the most popular fantasy trilogies of all time, and it's also one of the most well-known sequential series. In this series, each entry is a complete story in its own right, but is also connected to the larger fight to defeat the Dark Lord Sauron.

The first book, *The Fellowship of the Ring*, is a good example of this. In this book, the primary conflict is figuring out what to do with the One Ring, the source of Sauron's power. The characters are being hunted by his minions, but are also struggling with the Ring itself. Not just anyone can carry it, because they risk being corrupted by Sauron's will if they do. By the end of the book, this conflict is resolved when the Fellowship is formed and Frodo agrees to carry the Ring, setting out to destroy it once and for all—directly leading into the next book, which picks back up as their journey continues.

This is a bit different from something like *Dragon School*, which is a twenty-book episodic series.

For context, this story centers on a young girl named Amel as she struggles to join and survive Dragon School. Amel is disabled, and her world treats her as a burden because of that. Becoming a Dragon Rider is one of the only ways she can gain respect, but in doing so, she's pulled into a complex political struggle that threatens both her and the people she's come to care about.

Compared to *The Lord of the Rings*, the entries in this series are much, *much* shorter—usually only a novella in terms of length. The pacing is faster, and each episode picks up almost immediately after the last. Because of this, the books in this series tend to have a very narrow focus:

- In book one, Amel arrives at Dragon School and completes her initial test
- In the second, a week has passed, and students are studying for their first mission
- In the third, Amel and her friends head for the Ruby Isles, preparing for bigger battles
- In the fourth, a friend is kidnapped, and Amel starts to uncover hidden plots
- And so on…

All of this leads to a handful of key turning points (roughly every five books in the series), which add up to the larger finale of the story, one small bite at a time.

Though both of these examples build towards an overarching plot, they each approach it differently, depending on their series type.

Lessons from Chapter Two

At their core, sequential series aren't that different from standalone novels. They do have their own challenges and things to consider, but they follow most of the same rules, and will likely feel fairly natural for most writers.

Episodic series, though, are often a problem child.

Holding readers' attention in an episodic series is tricky, because you always need to create the sense that progress is being made—even when you're off gallivanting through side quests and subplots. This isn't always intuitive, and because of this, I find many episodic authors shy away from side stories entirely. Instead, they focus solely on their central plot, but in much smaller units.

Personally, I think this is kind of a shame. Part of the beauty of episodic series (and what sets them apart from sequential series) is how much flexibility you really have. Though this is a double-edged sword, it can have some serious benefits for both you and your story.

The key is understanding what you're giving your reader in each episode.

Early on, you'll likely want to stick close to your overarching plot, in order to give readers time to get invested in your characters, conflict, and world. Once that investment is there though, side stories are a good way to deepen readers' relationships with specific characters and have some fun with the story. So long as you don't stray from your overarching plot for too long, you can still maintain that sense of forward momentum that keeps the story alive.

Length has a role to play in this too. If each episode is a longer novella, readers might be less open to reading thirty thousand words that don't closely tie to your main plot. But, if your episodes are only a few thousands words, that resistance is much lower.

Both of these types of series are about striking a balance. Readers want to feel like they're moving towards something meaningful, alongside characters they love and a world they care about. If you give them that feeling, they should be more than happy to come along for the ride, no matter how many entries your series takes!

In the meantime, here are a few questions to help you apply what you've learned to your story:

- What is your overarching plot, and how does it develop across each book?
- How will your characters grow and change throughout the series?
- What smaller turning points can you build towards, whether as the finale of each book or as the end of a season of episodes?
- How will you create a flow throughout the series, so each entry feels like a natural extension of the story?

Once you've answered these questions, I'll see you in Chapter Three!

3

STATIC VS. ANTHOLOGY

A few months back, I was chatting with a student after teaching a workshop on plot. Throughout the class, we had talked a lot about how important it is to tie the threads of your story together in a rousing finale, whether you're writing a simple standalone or a larger series. The best stories build to something meaningful—and series allow you to do that on an even bigger scale.

The more we talked though, the more that student looked panicked.

After we wrapped up, I asked her what was on her mind, and she said she was struggling with the pressure of writing a huge series. She knew she wanted a series (and had plenty of ideas to go around), but trying to weave it all together into "the next *Game of Thrones*" felt basically impossible.

She was afraid she would never succeed as an author without emulating the epic series she was used to, but she also couldn't give up on the smaller stories she was dying to tell.

This is why I love teaching about static and anthology series —because for many writers, this might be the first time they're exposed to them. Unless you read in specific genres where these styles are the norm, it's easy to think that series are some rigid ideal.

In reality though, series encompass a lot of stories.

And not all of those have to be grand adventures that take decades to write!

The Static Series

To start, let's focus on static series.

Static series are the classic monster-of-the-week style series endemic to mysteries, crime novels, and thrillers. These series have no overarching plot, though some events from earlier books may shape the events or casts of later ones.

Instead, static series are just that—static.

Each novel follows the same protagonist as they face a variety of similar (but different) challenges. There might be a new murder to solve, a new crime syndicate to uncover, or a new shadowy threat to overthrow. Though the specifics of each book are unique, the core setup remains the same, providing a steady foundation from which to build a practically infinite number of stories.

This style of series is especially popular in mysteries and thrillers—though there are certainly examples of static series in other genres too.

For instance, consider something like *Jack Reacher* or *James Bond*. Each novel largely stands alone, meaning readers can pick up the series just as easily in book one as in book twenty-seven. Rather than tell some grand story, we instead get to experience heists, crimes, and capers with the same familiar hero and same familiar setup. Though 007's past may come back to haunt him occasionally, it's only really to provide flavor to an otherwise self-contained story.

STATIC SERIES STRUCTURE

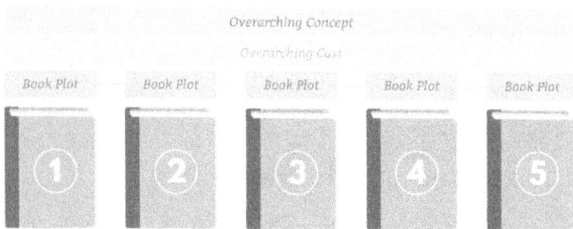

This is the beauty of static series!

Once you find a formula that works for you, you can iterate on that formula again and again, making space for smaller but still connected stories.

Of course, your novels still need to pull readers in. Your characters won't undergo a massive, series-long arc of change, and your plot won't slowly unfold across multiple books—meaning something else needs to keep them coming back for more. For most static series, that'll be a compelling world, an interesting mystery, or a hero they can't help but identify with.

When combined, the best static series fulfill a few things:

- They have a compelling concept or setup that repeats throughout the series
- The protagonist is engaging to read about, even if

they don't change from book to book
- They have an interesting cast of characters that come and go, keeping the series fresh
- And each entry honors the main promise of the series—whether that's a clever murder or a high-stakes mission

The Anthology Series

At the beginning of this book, I said that all series fall on a spectrum. Anthology series are by far the *farthest* end of that spectrum we've looked at yet.

Similar to static series, anthology series don't have an over-arching plot, but they don't have an overarching protagonist either. Instead, an anthology series is linked only by a common theme or setup, one that repeats across a variety of individual stories, unique protagonists, and (in extreme cases) even separate worlds.

ANTHOLOGY SERIES STRUCTURE

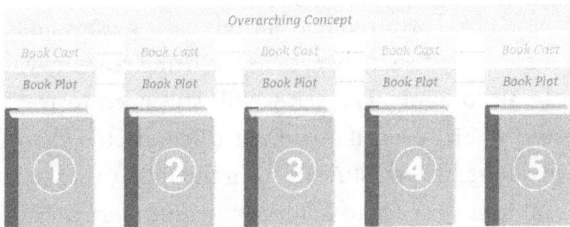

As you might imagine, this makes anthology series especially common in romance.

Romance as a genre typically requires a happily ever after at the end of each book, which makes continuing each entry tricky at best. Readers want to see the lovers get together in a clear and satisfying conclusion, both for the relationship and the story. So, how do you build a series when each book is well and truly "done" after the wedding bells ring?

Well, you tie them together in another way!

For many romance series, this is about a familiar location—perhaps each couple falls in love in the same picturesque beach town, or the same remote bed and breakfast. For others, they rely on the same trope, such as enemies-to-lovers or fake weddings. While in some, each protagonist is a sibling out to find true love, as you'll see in our case study in just a moment.

Anthology series aren't limited to romance, though. *The Graceling Realm* is an excellent fantasy anthology, as is the *Books of Bayern* series by Shannon Hale. Both of these series follow different protagonists in a common world, with only hints of the prior books woven throughout each entry.

This gives you the most flexibility of any type of series—but also the biggest challenge.

Each new novel will require entirely new heroes and plots, and that means it isn't always easy to bring readers with you from book to book. The series will still need to feel like a cohesive whole, even if it's more disconnected than most. Still (if you're like my student from the intro), this style does give you tons of space to tell really unique stories that might not otherwise fit in what's typically viewed as a "series."

Here are just a few of the ways you could connect an anthology series:

- **Common Setup:** Such as a stranger from the city falling for a dashing shopkeeper.

- **Common World:** Such as in Terry Pratchett's *Discworld* series.
- **Common Trope:** Such as a farm boy becoming king or a single bed gone awry.
- **Common Relationship:** Where each book follows one member of a family or friend group.
- **Common Theme:** Such as "the meaning of power" or "love conquers all."

Though all of these can work on their own, they become even stronger when you mix them together, combining into a series that fulfills a few key traits:

- They have a compelling concept or setup that repeats throughout the series
- They layer common worlds, tropes, or themes for maximum impact
- They're careful to respect (or at least consider) the expectations of readers
- And each entry honors the main promise of the series, no matter how different they seem

Case Study: Sherlock Holmes vs. Bridgerton

With all that in mind, let's take a closer look at how these two series types work in action.

First up, *Sherlock Holmes*.

This is one of the most famous examples of a static series ever created, following the titular "consulting detective" Holmes as he solves a variety of crimes. As a static series, each book stands alone, and focuses on a different mystery for Holmes to explore—though some events of earlier books are mentioned in (or have an influence on) later books.

Holmes himself doesn't change all that much throughout the series, either. Though he gains new relationships and sometimes learns a lesson or two, he's largely the same character in *A Study in Scarlet* as he is in *The Hound of the Baskervilles*. What makes this series interesting isn't his development as a character, but his addictive personality and the thrill of solving the case.

Bridgerton, in contrast, has no titular protagonist. Instead, it has an entire family.

In this anthology series, we follow eight siblings as they set out to find love and get married—or avoid getting married, depending on the book. Though we have a different protagonist and plot in each entry, there's no doubt this is a cohesive series. Beyond just the family connection, each book follows a similar setup in a similar world, neatly tying the whole thing together.

For instance, in *The Duke and I*, we follow Daphne Bridgerton during her fake courtship with Simon, which eventually ends in a very real marriage. Meanwhile, *The Viscount Who Loved Me* focuses on Daphne's older brother Anthony. In that book, he gets caught in an enemies-to-lovers relationship with Kate while trying (and failing) to court her sister.

While each book has its own lovers and its own spin, they still feel like part of a connected experience thanks to that overarching concept and family.

Lessons from Chapter Three

Ultimately, if you're considering writing either a static or anthology series, there's one big question you'll need to ask:

How much story do you really have to tell?

Because each entry in these series can stand alone, you have a lot more flexibility than with a sequential or episodic series. However, that also puts a bit more work on you. You can't simply expand on one long story, but instead need to craft smaller, connected stories to keep your series alive.

So, think carefully about where you want your series to go, and how long you want it to be. Build room for future novels into your original entry, whether in the form of a repeatable formula, a large family, or something else. There's a reason these two types of series are common in mysteries, thrillers, and romance. Those genres lend themselves to this style—though you certainly aren't limited by these if you have another story in mind.

Either way, aim to set yourself up for success from the start, so you can run with your series for as long as it excites you.

In the meantime, here are a few questions to help you apply what you've learned to your story:

- What overarching concept links your series together?
- How will you get readers attached to and identifying with your characters?
- Do you have enough ideas for individual (but connected) stories to support a full series?
- How will you ensure each entry feels like an exciting return to your story's world?

Once you've answered these questions, I'll see you in Chapter Four!

4

EXPLORING THE (EXTENDED)
UNIVERSE

Thus far, we've dug into a lot of examples, dropped plenty of names, and hopefully given you a structure within which to conceptualize your own fictional series.

But, what about the series that just don't fit? The ones built around a core trilogy, a few standalone novels, and maybe an anthology side series for good measure? Or the ones that are a weird blend of everything we've discussed, bucking every trend and with no easy logic in sight?

You know... Those series!

Though it might give my organizer brain migraines, series *are* a spectrum, and not every series will cleanly fit in the categories we've been exploring. However, nine times out of ten they will, and the ones that don't likely *do* when you peer a bit closer thanks to what's called an extended universe.

Stretching Beyond a Series

The idea of extended universes has become increasingly popular in recent years, though it's far from a new concept. Many of our examples from this book have come from extended universes, from *The Lord of the Rings* to the *Discworld* series.

These days though, extended universes are rapidly entering the public lexicon, thanks in large part to the rise of comic book adaptations. This style of series has always been popular in comics—and as the Marvel Cinematic Universe has dominated the box office for over a decade, it's also encouraged more and more authors to build extended universes of their own.

So, how exactly does this work?

Basically, an extended universe is a group of series or standalone novels set in a common fictional world. Each series is complete in its own right and follows the basic structures we've discussed, but is also linked in other ways. Characters might transfer over, concepts and worldbuilding from one series will shape the others, and the result is a wide net of stories (or graphic novels, games, movies, and comics) all existing under the same canonical umbrella.

An example I'm sure you're familiar with is *Star Wars*.

This extended universe began with a single film trilogy, telling a complete sequential story across three movies. But, as the series gained in popularity, there was a push for more. Soon we had multiple core film trilogies, as well as dozens of novels, shows, and other supplemental material all set in the same universe.

Of course, there are plenty of other ways extended universes could manifest too. For instance, *The Hunger Games* recently crossed into extended universe territory by releasing a standalone prequel to the original trilogy. Other extended universes might pair a sequential series with an anthology series, or an episodic series with a short static series.

This is what makes extended universes so fascinating. There are almost limitless combinations, opening the door to a huge variety of stories woven together into a single, massive "universe."

Case Study: The Grishaverse

If you're curious how this works in action, look no further than Leigh Bardugo's Grishaverse.

This extended universe began with the *Shadow and Bone* trilogy, a YA fantasy series which established the common world each future entry would take place in. It introduced us to key mechanics, set up a deep history, and got us used to the rules and dangers future characters would face.

From there, the universe has expanded with two additional duologies: *Six of Crows* and *King of Scars*.

Six of Crows focuses on a new protagonist in an entirely new country, but is linked to the prior trilogy through that common world. The same goes for *King of Scars*, which returns to the kingdom featured in *Shadow and Bone*, but many years later. On the surface, these duologies aren't directly linked. But, that common world makes them feel familiar and connected to readers.

Toss in a handful of supplemental standalones and a recent graphic novel (not to mention a Netflix adaptation), and you can start to see how that initial series has blossomed and grown. Each new entry works on its own and fits within the series structures we've explored. They're satisfying, worthwhile stories even without picking up the entire universe— but there's no denying that that universe adds a whole new layer for dedicated readers to dig into.

The Risks of a Universe

Of course, extended universes involve trade-offs just like any series type.

To pull off an extended universe, you need a strong core series to establish your world and get readers invested. This is the entry point for readers new to your work, and gives them a stable launchpad into the rest of your stories.

You'll also need enough material to support multiple related series. For some authors this is a large cast of characters, while for others it's deep mechanics, an expansive continent, or a complex history.

Either way, you should think of extended universes almost like anthology series.

Just like an anthology series involves individual stories linked by an overarching concept (and sometimes not much else), an extended universe involves multiple series linked by the same. This means your worldbuilding and characters are incredibly important here. Your side characters need enough depth to potentially support spin-off series of their own, and your world needs to feel vibrant and satisfying for readers to exist in.

You need to feel excited about your universe too. Writing a series is a big commitment, but writing a universe could be a lifelong one. If you aren't bursting at the seams with interesting ideas to fill out this catalog, it may be a hard thing to sustain for the long run.

Fortunately, you can always expand on an existing series later if that changes—and if you manage to build a truly lasting universe, the benefits are well worth it! Readers who stick around are likely to become dedicated fans for years to come, and will be some of the biggest advocates for your work. You're not just giving them a single series here, but a whole world for them to live in and love. Just look at Brandon Sanderson's record-breaking Kickstarter to see how deep this loyalty can go, *if* you treat your readers well.

Lessons from Chapter Four

Extended universes represent a more complicated side of series, and they also highlight just how varied the world of storytelling can be.

Is a video game part of a series? What about a graphic novel, a movie, or a collection of short stories? Can a board game be part of your series canon, and just how far can you expand while still creating a meaningful connection?

For most authors, this is more than they want to deal with— but for others, this is an exciting opportunity to really push the limits of their writing abilities. Wherever you fall in this debate, the key is knowing how you'll juggle all the pieces of your story, extended universe or not.

We've really just scratched the surface of everything you need to consider when writing a fictional series, but don't worry! As we move into Part Two, it's time to take the structures we've discussed and see how they'll actually shape the unique stories you have to tell.

In the meantime, here are a few questions to help you apply what you've learned to your story:

- If you want to write an extended universe, how far can you realistically stretch your story into a string of interconnected series?
- Are your ideas all linked by a common universe?
- Are you comfortable dedicating your focus to a single world, potentially for decades?

Once you've answered these questions, I'll see you in Chapter Five!

II

THE BIGGER PICTURE

"Ideas are like rabbits. You get a couple and learn how to handle them, and pretty soon you have a dozen."

JOHN STEINBECK

5

CHOOSING YOUR PATH

Have you ever stood in a store paralyzed by seemingly endless options?

This happened to me just recently when trying to buy BBQ sauce, of all things. My local grocery store doesn't just have a shelf for BBQ sauce—they have half an aisle. There were probably fifty different brands and varieties to choose from, from vinegar-based to tomato-based, sweet sauces to smoky sauces, and even a few pineapple ones (sorry, not a fan).

Quite frankly, it was all too much to process.

Analysis paralysis is a frustrating part of life, where you feel so overwhelmed by everything you *could* be doing, that you can't decide *what* to do. In my case, this was whether to buy Sweet Baby Ray's or Stubb's. But, depending on how much you already knew going into this book, for you it might be choosing your series type.

For many authors, the type of series they want to write is clear from the beginning, especially if they're writing in a genre dominated by one style or the other. However, it's also possible the last few chapters introduced you to options you didn't know you had.

This isn't limited to your series type either. You'll also need to decide how much story you have to tell, how long your series will be, and what best fits your goals as an author.

So, before you move forward, we have some choices to make!

What Are You Writing?

If you're looking towards the future and thinking about how you'll eventually publish your series, it can be tempting to feel limited by what's "normal."

Every genre has certain expectations around what a series looks like. These have been built over decades, and are rooted in what readers are used to seeing. Science fiction is full of sequential series, while romances are almost universally anthology series, and thrillers are usually static series.

Yet, I'd argue "writing to market" shouldn't be your first concern when choosing your series type.

Plenty of series reject genre norms to great success, because that story was truly served by a different series structure. Instead, this should be part of a much larger discussion, one where you consider both the story you want to tell *and* the expectations of your future readers.

———

Your Story Itself:

Most of us start writing because we're inspired. Some small idea has taken root in our minds, and as it grows, it morphs into a basic story. Though this idea might have holes and room for improvement, there's still a central vision driving it —one you need to honor as you plan your fictional series.

That's why, to choose your series type, I encourage you to start with your story itself:

- **Your Overarching Concept:** What overarching concept ties your series together? Is it a grand plot, a familiar hero, or a common setup? This is often the easiest way to determine your series type, since each style approaches this differently.
- **Your Series Finale:** How do you envision your plot? Are you building up to a large, epic finale, or are you exploring smaller, separate adventures? Sequential and episodic series lend themselves to grand conclusions, while static and anthology series iterate on the same idea in each entry.
- **Subplots and Side Quests:** Do you have lots of side stories to explore? Do you have a bunch of characters with their own adventures to go on? While sequential series tend to be focused on the main plot, episodic, static, and anthology series have a bit more room for flexibility.
- **Your Protagonist:** Will you explore a new protagonist in each novel, or dig deep into a single hero? Though sequential and episodic series may have ensemble casts or multiple protagonists, you still get a consistent hero throughout the series. Same goes for static series, while anthology series change protagonists in each entry.

Depending on how fleshed out your ideas are, you might not know the answer to some of these questions, and that's ok. None of these options are bad. They're just different! Sit back and daydream about how your series would change depending on the structure you follow, and see what speaks to you. Talk to friends, brainstorm with a critique partner, and try to get a sense of the story you most want to tell.

Your Future Readers:

Once you've spent some time on your story itself, you can consider your readers.

Readers of different genres have different expectations, based on what's normal for those stories. This means certain genres mesh better with some types of series than others.

Take fantasy, for example. Sequential series are incredibly common in the fantasy genre, so much so that many fantasy readers would be surprised to pick up a static or anthology series. Romance is the opposite. Romance series are almost all anthology, since the "will they, won't they" conflict is the real hook of the story—one that needs to be resolved at the end of each novel.

While there are no hard rules, here are some types of series common in different genres:

- **Fantasy:** Sequential, episodic, sometimes anthology.
- **Sci-Fi:** Sequential, episodic, sometimes anthology.
- **Romance:** Typically anthology, rarely sequential.
- **Thriller:** Static, sometimes anthology.
- **Mystery:** Static, sometimes anthology.
- **Historical:** Sequential and anthology.

You might notice that almost all of these have multiple options, and that's because there's more flexibility here than you might assume. Though each genre has one series type that dominates, there are always outliers that manage to tell amazing, successful stories in unusual ways. So long as you're careful to consider what readers are looking for from your series, this doesn't have to restrict your creativity.

Your Reasons for Writing:

All of this raises a question: Why are you writing this series?

If this is just a pet project, genre be damned—but for most authors, we write to be read. We want readers to love our stories, and though you'll never please everyone, it's still important to think about what your ideal reader is looking for. Bucking trends and ignoring conventions *will* drive readers away. Sometimes, removing the friction of an unexpected series structure is the best way to get readers on board, so you can surprise (and delight) them later on.

For career authors who really do write to market, that makes this decision fairly easy. But regardless of your publishing goals, it's worth thinking about what you want out of your series when all is said and done.

Depending on your answer, you should have a better idea of your ideal series type.

———

In the end, the choice is yours. But, I encourage you to make this choice with care, no matter what path you decide to take. Writing is a balancing act, and when it comes to structuring your series, that balance is somewhere between the story in your head and the readers you hope will love it.

The Question of Length

Of course, your series type may be the biggest factor in shaping your series—but there is one other element that will play a role in your series' final form.

And that is your length.

This can be a bit of guesswork, especially at this early stage. Your decision might change over time, and that's ok. What started as a short, four-book static series could always take off, turning into a ten, fifteen, or even twenty-book behemoth before it's all through.

Still, it's worth considering before you dive into writing your series. Knowing how many books you have to work with provides a lot of clarity, and ensures you're taking your stamina into account when planning the story. Writing a trilogy is very different from writing a twelve-book fantasy epic, after all!

Though series come in a huge number of lengths, here are a few ranges to guide your decision.

———

Duologies (Two Books):

Duologies are almost exclusively the domain of sequential series. This is a nice, condensed way to write a series that's becoming increasingly popular in fantasy, science fiction, and young adult fiction. Because you only have to stretch your story across two novels, it's easier to coax readers over into your second book, and it also lends itself well to a strong book one cliffhanger.

If your story involves any kind of false victory or surprise twist right in the middle, this could be a sign to consider a duology.

Trilogies (Three Books):

The gold standard of sequential series in particular, trilogies are common in basically all series types. Readers like sets of three—and so do authors!

Writing a trilogy gives you plenty of room to tell a grander story, while still being manageable to actually complete in a timely fashion. They have their own energy and cadence, and they're an incredibly fun way to craft a story. We'll chat more about trilogies in Chapter Nine, but for now, just know that this is a classic for good reason.

4-6 Book Series:

A happy middle common in all types of series.

This is definitely substantial, but it's still far from gigantic. You'll need dedicated readers to stick around until the end, but if you can pull it off, this is a great length for building a loyal fan base no matter what style of series you're writing.

7-12 Book Series:

We're getting pretty long here, and because of that, this length is more common in static, anthology, and episodic series. At the high end of this range, you'll need an expansive story to keep the series moving, or at least a compelling overarching concept you can iterate on from book to book.

Though some sequential series hit this length, it can definitely be a challenge.

12+ Book Series:

Almost exclusively the domain of static, episodic, and anthology series (or extended universes, such as Terry Pratchett's forty-one-book *Discworld* series).

The hardest part of a series this long is keeping readers invested, especially if they have to read every book in order to follow the story. Since static and anthology series can be started at any point, this is less of a concern, hence why they're more common at this length.

———

Much like when choosing your series type, I'd argue your first concern here should be the story you have to tell—specifically, the *amount* of story.

I strongly discourage you from trying to pad out your series in order to fill an arbitrary number of books. Though this can work out, most of the time, readers can feel when an author has run out of ideas. Instead, consider how long the average novel is in your genre. What's the scope of your vision, and how many books would you need to realize it?

A professor of mine told me many years ago that a good thesis paper should be "as long as it needs to be, and no longer." Though we're not dealing with footnotes and bibliographies here, the same sentiment applies. Perhaps a duology is a better fit for your story, rather than a more traditional trilogy. Or maybe your short static series can support way more books than you originally thought, opening room for you to expand on it later.

Then there's the elephant in the room: Standalone novels.

Though this is a book on writing series, it would be remiss of me to ignore the reality that some stories are really best suited for standalone novels. There's nothing wrong with that—it just means the story is more focused, maybe has fewer characters, and would feel artificial if you stretched it any further.

Other novels simply have a clear end. Even if you wanted to expand them into a longer series, the story has reached its natural conclusion, and there's something to be said for respecting that. Perhaps another idea would fit a series better.

Whatever the case is for you, don't be afraid to honor the length that feels right for your series. Again, there's a balance here! Whether you're writing one book or twenty, you can still tell a riveting and successful story.

NOTE: If you're reading this book because you already have a standalone novel and want to turn it into a series, don't worry! We'll discuss your situation specifically in Part Three.

Lessons from Chapter Five

No matter what series type you choose, all of your decisions from here on out will weave back to this point. Your series structure will determine the shape of your plot. It'll influence how your characters grow (or not). And it'll even shape your writing process and book launches.

Because of this, don't be afraid to take your time with these decisions. Consider what each path would look like for your story, and be open to options you might not have thought of before.

Once you're confident in your vision of your story, *then* we can chat about all the other parts of writing a series!

In the meantime, here are a few questions to help you apply what you've learned to your story:

- What is your vision for your story, and how does that align with one of the four series types?
- What genre are you writing in, and what's the norm for series in that genre?
- How much stamina and patience do you have to stick with a long-running series?
- What is your series' natural end point, where the story feels truly complete?

Once you've answered these questions, I'll see you in Chapter Six!

6

WHAT ABOUT PLOT?

When it comes to sitting down and actually writing your series, plot is one of those things that most writers get a bit panicked about.

I've had conversations with dozens of writers over the years where the thought of building a complex, interconnected plot was like a dark storm cloud. There's this sense that you need to write some behemoth of a story, weaving in plot threads and foreshadowing that won't even be *mentioned* again until book eight or beyond.

However, depending on the type of series you're writing, you might have a much easier time than you think.

Static and anthology series have no connected plot, meaning they follow the same general rules as any standalone novel. So long as you honor the overarching concept we've talked so much about, you can plan each entry in your series basically on its own.

The difficult ones are sequential and episodic series.

These series do rely on both book-specific plots and a larger, overarching plot—and both need to be tightly linked for your series to succeed. This isn't an easy feat, but it's not an impossible one either. There are lots of tools you can use to make this easier, and to give yourself the kind of thirty-thousand-foot view that lets you make sense of your story.

Because of this, we won't be focusing much on static and anthology series in this chapter. There are plenty of great resources on plot for standalone novels that will serve you well if you're in either of those camps.

Instead, this chapter will be about the intersection of that book-specific plot and your overarching plot. It's a careful dance, but one that doesn't have to be as frightening as you might think!

Planning Your Dual Plots

To start, let me recap the two components of a series from back in Chapter One:

- **The Book-Specific Plot:** The individual plot of each book in the series, similar to a standalone novel. This plot follows all the same rules as any other story, to ensure each novel is satisfying to read even though it's only one part of a larger tale.
- **The Overarching Concept:** The big idea (often in the form of a larger plot, cast, or conflict) that links every book in the series. This stretches from beginning to end, and binds the series together as a cohesive whole.

For sequential and episodic series specifically, that overarching concept will come in the form of your plot. Each novel in the series will be a building block, slowly adding together into a larger, grander story that stretches across every book you write.

This means that pacing is incredibly important for these types of series.

You're not just holding readers' attention across eight thousand words—you're holding it across multiple *novels*. This means each novel needs to feel like it's making progress towards your big finale. It has to say something, trigger some change in your story, and end in a way that pulls readers into your next book.

The best way to approach this is through what's called story structure.

If you've spent much time in the writing world, you're likely familiar with this concept. Story structures are frameworks writers use to create riveting plots, allowing them to pace the events of their story for maximum impact. This applies to all types of novels—but in the case of sequential and episodic series, this structure also applies at the series level. Not only will you have a structure within each book, but each book will act as one point along your larger series plot.

There are dozens of well-established story structures out there, so if you're a nerd about this like I am, you have lots to choose from. However, for the sake of this book, I'd like to give you a quick primer on the structure I use in my work as an editor, called the Four Act Structure.

This structure is built around four phases, each with a specific role in the story:

- **Act One (Setup):** A chance for you to set the stage. During this act, you'll introduce readers to your characters, plot, and world, and light the spark that will become your central conflict. This helps readers get invested in the story.

- **Act Two (Struggle):** A period of reaction and learning, where your protagonist struggles to get their bearings in the new world created by your conflict. They'll adapt, make friends and enemies, and slowly uncover the true nature of your plot.

- **Act Three (Pursuit):** With a new plan in hand, it's time to take action. Here your hero will focus on resolving your conflict using everything they've learned thus far. However, there are cracks beneath the surface. This act ends with a major defeat, throwing their plans into question.

- **Act Four (Climax):** Finally, your protagonist will have a chance to recover, gather their wits, and resolve your plot once and for all. Depending on the arc of their story, they'll either succeed or fail, creating lasting consequences in their life and world.

Alongside these, you'll also have four crossroads, which serve as key turning points that link your protagonist's journey as a character with the larger conflict of your plot. Each act will end with its corresponding crossroad, almost like a miniature finale. This slowly builds until the Fourth Crossroad, which resolves your plot and leads into the Resolution:

- **The First Crossroad:** The first major decision your hero makes, dragging them into the conflict. This pushes them past a point of no return, embroiling them in your plot and beginning their journey.

- **The Second Crossroad:** A major test. Here your protagonist will face a difficult challenge and make another key decision. They leverage everything they've learned up until now to succeed, though not without lingering problems and weaknesses.

- **The Third Crossroad:** Another challenge arises, this time with darker consequences. Here your protagonist falls back into old habits, triggering a dark night of the soul. They fail in a big way, and their plans are thrown awry.
- **The Fourth Crossroad:** Your finale. Here your protagonist will experience one final test, demanding that they embrace the lessons they've learned to succeed. If they do so, they'll resolve the conflict of your story and cement their growth as a character.

Beneath all of this is your core conflict, which is the primary obstacle, challenge, or threat that underpins your novel. This is the real lifeblood of good storytelling (no matter what type of story you're writing), and it drives your characters to take action, face risks, and create the kind of emotional investment that keeps readers on the page. It's the glue that binds your plot, characters, and world together—thus giving your novel a reason to exist.

This is a *very* high-level view of this structure, and skips over a few smaller plot points and nuances we simply don't have time for here. Still, this should be enough for you to see how your plot could unfold across your series.

Depending on the type of series you're writing, this will play out in one of two ways:

———

Sequential Series Plots:

When writing a sequential series, your overarching plot will be your primary focus in every novel. Even if you're writing a longer series (anywhere from five to twelve novels), each entry will be a substantial length, meaning they need to trigger serious developments in your story to keep readers invested.

All of this hinges on that core conflict I just mentioned. Unlike, say, a static series where there is no larger conflict connecting each book, a sequential series relies on that bigger threat to tie the story together. In something like *The Lord of the Rings*, that's the threat of Sauron, which is resolved when the One Ring is destroyed in the final book. Same goes for *The Hunger Games* series, which focuses on the oppressive Capitol and the rebellion against it.

This means each novel will have its own plot, while also fulfilling key structural moments within your series.

Here's how this would work for a four-book series:

- **Book One (A1):** Sets the stage with an initial conflict and introduction. Ends with the First Crossroad.
- **Book Two (A2):** Begins to explore the larger scope of the series. Ends with the Second Crossroad.
- **Book Three (A3):** A low moment, where your heroes face their biggest challenge yet. Ends with the Third Crossroad.
- **Book Four (A4):** The finale of the story, where all of your plot threads come together. Ends with the Fourth Crossroad and a look towards the future.

Of course, this is pretty cut-and-dry, since each book aligns with one of the four acts. So, here's an alternative setup using a six-book sequential series:

- **Book One (A1):** Sets the stage with an initial conflict and introduction. Ends with the First Crossroad.
- **Book Two (A2) :** Begins to explore the larger scope of the series.
- **Book Three (A2):** A test of your characters, and a chance for them to prove themselves. Ends with the Second Crossroad.
- **Book Four (A3):** Your cast is flexing their new skills, but there's still a threat lingering over them.
- **Book Five (A3):** A low moment, where your heroes face their biggest challenge yet. Ends with the Third Crossroad.
- **Book Six (A4):** The finale of the story, where all of your plot threads come together. Ends with the Fourth Crossroad and a look towards the future.

Both of these are just examples, so you will need to consider the specifics of your situation. Still, no matter how long your sequential series is, try to spread these crossroads evenly across each book. That way, there's never too much of a gap between major turning points, keeping the momentum high and your readers engaged in the larger story.

We'll chat about trilogies in a later chapter.

Episodic Series Plots:

Next up, episodic series work similarly to sequential series, in that they're still linked by that larger overarching plot. However, whereas sequential series are tightly focused, episodic ones have a bit more room for exploration.

On the surface, both styles of series follow the same rules and structure. You'll still need a strong grasp on your core conflict, and you'll still be building towards that grand finale. However, you're working in smaller chunks, often of only a few thousand words. This leaves room for side quests and subplots, meaning some books in the series might only tangentially relate to your overarching plot.

Here's what this could look like across a ten-book series:

- **Book One (A1):** Setup, introducing us to the world and characters with an initial conflict.
- **Book Two (A1):** A new trial, showing us the true threat of the story. Ends with the First Crossroad.
- **Book Three (A2):** Time to explore this new world and everything in store.
- **Book Four (A2):** Side quest, looping back to the overarching plot at the end.
- **Book Five (A2):** Building towards an exciting reveal. Ends with the Second Crossroad.
- **Book Six (A3):** A chance to plan and prepare as your characters start coming into their own.
- **Book Seven (A3):** Side quest, looping back to the overarching plot at the end.
- **Book Eight (A3):** A painful defeat, throwing the future into question. Ends with the Third Crossroad.
- **Book Nine (A4):** Recovery, where your hero discovers a path forward.
- **Book Ten (A4):** The series finale, when everything reaches its peak. Ends with the Fourth Crossroad.

There is one more point to keep in mind here, and that's the idea of season arcs.

Because episodic series can be so long, many authors choose to organize them into smaller "seasons" within the larger series. Each season has its own plot, side quests, arc, and finale, and builds up to the full series.

Honestly, this kind of blurs the line between episodic series and extended universes, and works best for series that are already extremely long. Seasons are almost like tiny series in their own right, and can become pretty meta pretty quickly —but still, it's worth considering as you plan your series plot.

So long as each book loops back to your core conflict and you don't go too long without a bigger turning point, you can keep the momentum going for dozens of novels!

———

If you remember nothing else from these examples, the one thing you'll hopefully notice is that each of these hypothetical books leads into the next.

This is because each novel needs to create an "open loop."

You don't want to leave readers hanging at the end of a book (more on cliffhangers in a second), but you do want them asking questions about where your series will go next. What about that new character who was acting suspicious? Or that strange letter our heroes received? Will the growing rebellion ignite in the next book, or will we finally see the five kingdoms reunite?

By leaving them with the sense that the story isn't done, you invite them into the next book, and make it much less likely they'll fall off the series.

Where Should Each Book End?

That brings us to one last question: How do you decide where one book ends and the next begins?

With sequential and episodic series, the lines between books can often feel blurry. Even I describe these series as one long story that couldn't fit in a single novel, which makes it hard to know where each entry should shift into the next.

The answer to this once again lies in story structure. As I mentioned earlier, your series will be built around a core conflict, which drives your overarching plot. However, each of your novels will also have their own book-specific conflict. This is a smaller stepping stone within your larger series—and once it's resolved, the story enters a lull, forming a natural end to that book.

By resolving that book-specific conflict, you give readers a satisfying conclusion, without cutting the series short. There are still questions to ask and problems to solve, but for now, they get the enjoyment of a clear finale. *The Fellowship of the Ring* ends when Sam and Frodo escape with the One Ring. *The Hunger Games* ends when Katniss and Peeta outsmart the Capitol. And *Outlander* ends when Claire and Jamie escape to safety in France. All of these books have more story to tell as their respective series unfold, but their endings feel meaningful nonetheless.

They also don't end on cliffhangers.

Writers will often force readers through their series by ending each novel with a cliffhanger. On the surface, this makes some sense. The assumption is that readers will keep reading to find out what happens next, thus pulling them through the series.

Honestly though, cliffhangers usually do more harm than good.

Don't get me wrong—these have their place, and they're a tool every author should be familiar with. But, when used poorly, they deny readers the satisfaction of a clear conclusion. That satisfaction is why we read, and without it, we'll often feel like part of the story is missing. The author creates an explosion, but refuses to let us hear the "bang" that follows. Or they push a beloved character out the window, but don't show us the dashing firefighter that saves them at the last minute. It's emotionally exhausting, and not something that will endear readers to your series.

However, this doesn't mean you can't write a cliffhanger!

Despite that rather harsh review, cliffhangers have their place when used carefully, linking back to that "open loop" we talked about earlier. The key here is that you want to resolve the book-specific conflict you've set up, even as you leave a cliffhanger in your larger series conflict.

For example, say you're writing a mystery. You might show your protagonist being saved by the firefighter, thus allowing them to catch the killer trying to cover their tracks and resolving the core conflict of that book. But, in the final scene, you might also deliver a letter—the killer has escaped, and knows who foiled their plan. Now we have an even bigger problem afoot, leaving us with both a resolution of that book's plot, and an interesting cliffhanger to pull us into the next entry.

By introducing some new twist or larger obstacle, you let readers wonder about what might come next, but you still give them the immediate answers they're craving. This middle ground leaves them satisfied *and* intrigued. Compare that to stopping just short of your finale, and you can hopefully see why it's a more effective option.

Every story has a natural end point, one worth respecting. You just need to trust that your series is good enough to keep readers coming back for more!

Lessons from Chapter Six

This was a pretty dense chapter, but I hope it helped the plot of your series start to click in your mind. So long as you know the basic shape of your overarching plot, everything else is simply a matter of piecing the puzzle together.

Of course, all of this is specific to sequential and episodic series. Static and anthology series are much less complex, and much more like standalone novels.

There is one thing I hope you'll walk away with though, regardless of your series type.

No matter what style of series you're writing, knowing your core conflict is paramount. This conflict will drive your whole story, meaning the clearer it is, the easier it will be for you to write a novel worth reading. We talked a lot about how this works for sequential and episodic series, but it matters for static and anthology series too. Though there won't be one big, overarching conflict, there will be themes. Some series will be about catching the killer, others about finding true love, et cetera.

Whether static or sequential, knowing the conflict you're writing about is the first step to crafting a read-worthy plot.

In the meantime, here are a few questions to help you apply what you've learned to your story:

- What core conflict (or type of conflict) will underpin your series?

- What crossroads exist in your overarching plot, and where do they fall in each book?
- Are these crossroads evenly spread throughout the series, at least within reason?
- Do you raise the stakes as you progress through the Four Act Structure?

Once you've answered these questions, I'll see you in Chapter Seven!

7

YOUR SERIES CHARACTERS

One of the greatest joys of reading is getting to see the characters you love grow and change. It really creates the feeling that you're going on a journey, facing tests and trials that push you both to your limit and bring you closer together by the time they're all through.

And in a series, these emotions are only heightened.

Because your series stretches across a much larger span of time (both in your story itself and in your reader's life), readers have more chances to grow attached to your cast, and you have more space to craft unique, meaningful journeys. Depending on the scope of your series, they might have spent a literal lifetime with your characters—which means, in the final moments of that final book, you have the power to create one of the highest highs possible in storytelling.

Of course, this level of impact requires a deft hand and a strong grasp on writing, especially because series change how many characters are written. You don't just have a single story to worry about. Instead, you need to craft a cohesive journey for your cast, one that ebbs and flows through each novel you write.

So, while this book isn't a manual on character development, let's take a quick look at your series characters.

NOTE: If you want a deeper dive into writing strong protagonists, developing a cast, and creating character arcs, I highly recommend the first two books in this series: *Write Your Hero* and *Mastering Character Arcs*. This chapter will give you a primer on the subject, but those books will take you to the next level.

Character Arcs 101

Much like plot, characters interact differently in a series than in a standalone. Depending on the type of series you're writing, they might undergo one big transformation, but they could also face a string of smaller, connected challenges. Either way, this needs to feel consistent. Who they are in book twelve should be a logical extension of who they were in book one, and readers should be able to trace their growth through every entry in the series.

Fortunately, there's an easy tool to help you manage this, called character arcs.

Character arcs are similar to story structure, in that they're a framework writers use to craft characters that change believably across a story. In its simplest form, an arc is just the internal transformation of a character as they struggle to overcome major flaws or wounds. Much like your plot, this will be built around a few key turning points, as well as two important things:

- **The Harmful Belief:** A deeply held belief your character has about themselves or their world. Sometimes called their lie or their inner struggle, this belief prevents them from achieving their goals and resolving the core conflict of your novel.
- **The Lesson:** The new belief your character needs to learn. This stands in direct contrast to their harmful belief, making this the "message" of their story. Accepting this lesson is the final test of their arc.

How these beliefs interact is what will really determine your character's arc. This is where things become a bit complicated, but for the sake of this book, there are only three arcs you need to know:

- **The Positive Arc:** An arc about growth. Here your character starts out suffering from some harmful belief, faces tests and trials, and ultimately accepts an important lesson. It's through this lesson that they overcome their old beliefs and resolve the conflict of their story.
- **The Negative Arc:** An arc focused on decay. Here your character also starts out suffering from some harmful belief, but rather than overcome it, they succumb to it. They refuse to embrace their lesson and thus devolve into a worse version of themselves, leaving them unable to resolve the conflict of their story.
- **The Flat Arc:** An arc about teaching. Flat arc characters already know their lesson when their story begins. Rather than struggling to grow as an

individual, their arc is about sharing their lesson
with others, thus healing their world's harmful belief.

The way these apply to your series is the really fun part!

Most discussions of character arcs are rooted in standalone novels or perhaps sequential series. However, static, episodic, and anthology series all shape your cast in their own ways. This is especially apparent when it comes to your protagonist, making their arc the best way to see this in action.

———

Sequential Series Protagonists:

First up, sequential series.

Because this style tells one large story across a handful of full-length novels, your protagonist's arc will need to stretch throughout the series. This perfectly mirrors the crossroads we discussed in the previous chapter. If you remember, those crossroads are turning points for your plot, but also for your hero. Here they'll make a big decision that propels the story forward, while also showing readers how they're changing as a person.

It's this string of decisions that grounds their character arc, and that slowly builds to the Fourth Crossroad of the series, where they'll cement their transformation through action.

For example, consider a character named Marcus.

In the first book of the series, Marcus is bitter and jaded about the state of the world. However, by the end of that first book, his new experiences and allies help him realize that there's hope for the future. This carries him into book two, where he struggles to reconcile his newfound hope with his earlier experiences. Old relationships resurface, past wounds are tested, and he learns that hope isn't enough—to make the world a better place, you have to take action. This culminates in the third and final book, where Marcus fights to prove his new lesson and resolve the conflict of the series.

Each entry in the series marks a period of growth (and has its own book-specific character arc), but adds up to the larger arc of the whole series.

Episodic Series Protagonists:

Much like a sequential series, an episodic series will focus on character arcs that stretch across the entire story. However, because this style is built on much shorter installments, not every novel needs a full, book-specific arc. Instead, they might contain just pieces of a larger arc, or a string of season arcs that link groups of books within the series.

To illustrate this, take Marcus' distant cousin, Amina.

Just like Marcus, Amina starts her series bitter and jaded, with little hope for the future. As the series unfolds and her arc progresses though, she slowly finds a newfound sense of purpose, pushing her to fight for what's right as she faces the conflict of her story.

The difference is in how that story unfolds.

In book one, she might demonstrate her jaded mindset and have it challenged for the first time, but not learn a major lesson. In books two and three, this leads to new trials that call her beliefs into question, building into book four, where she embraces hope for the first time. Books five and six show her struggle to reconcile her past with her new perspective, and book seven ends on a painful defeat that calls her world into question. Finally, book eight is the culmination of her arc and her story, following her as she gets back up to fight for what's right, proving her growth as a character.

Static Series Protagonists:

Moving into static series, this style handles character arcs unlike any other—specifically, because there are none.

That's a bit of a strong statement, but it is mostly true. Since static series focus on a single protagonist facing different, isolated conflicts in each entry, static series heroes are just that. *Static.* They don't undergo a massive character arc in each book, and are instead consistent in their personality and beliefs, with only small changes across the series.

Instead, static series tend to focus on the arcs of secondary characters, as well as how the protagonist shapes those characters. This may mean that protagonist has a flat arc, but more often than not, they really have no arc at all. They're a round character, one fully developed with complex emotions and traits, but who doesn't undergo a substantial transformation across each book. They provide support and guidance for those around them, but are otherwise fairly consistent.

A possible example of this would be a character like Janet.

Janet is a consistently hopeful, optimistic character no matter what life throws at her—though she does have moments where doubt or fear creeps in, keeping her on her toes as she navigates life. In book one, she meets Nancy, a bitter and jaded woman frustrated by the state of the world. The two end up working together to resolve the conflict of that story, ending with Janet helping Nancy accept her lesson that small acts of kindness can change the world. This continues in each subsequent book, where Janet meets a new set of characters who grow and change, while Janet remains steady and stable.

Anthology Series Protagonists:

Last but not least, anthology series are often the easiest to handle, in that they're the most like a standalone novel.

In this style, the protagonist of each book will undergo their own book-specific character arc—at least before the series moves on to the next entry, and thus a new hero. Because of this, you have lots of flexibility to explore a variety of arcs, though they'll usually focus on the same primary theme. You don't have to stretch your hero across the entire series, so things are a bit easier to manage.

For instance, take Cadence.

Cadence is the protagonist of the first book in an anthology series, and starts out jaded and bitter about the world. Fortunately, as her story unfolds, she learns to embrace the future, allowing her to accept the love of other people. From there, we shift to Benedict, the protagonist of book two. Benedict undergoes a similar arc, but rather than starting out jaded due to past events, he grows more bitter as his story unfolds. He's forced to give up on his dreams by the novel's conflict, and only recovers by learning that he can chart his own destiny.

This pattern would repeat throughout the series, each with a new (and slightly different) hero.

———

As you can probably see, your protagonist is the central character of your story, and will thus be the most affected by your series. They're the clearest window into your world, meaning their thoughts, feelings, fears, and beliefs will play the largest role in shaping your readers' experience.

This means that your protagonist will almost always have an arc—barring static protagonists, which are a unique case.

Case Study: Essun vs. Jack Reacher

We've gone through quite a few hypothetical examples in this chapter, but I do want to leave you with one more look at how your series type will shape your characters.

First for this case study is Essun, the protagonist of the *Broken Earth* trilogy.

Essun lives on an apocalyptic version of Earth, one beset by cataclysms that have reshaped mankind. Her arc begins in book one, when her daughter is kidnapped. Essun has unique powers that allow her to manipulate the Earth, and her children have inherited those powers. This leads to her son being murdered and her daughter being taken from her, and so she sets out to find her. Essun's life thus far has left her bitter and angry, enraged by the abuse she's suffered because of her abilities—and this only grows throughout that first book. By the end of book one, she's fierce and driven, out to destroy the system that's hurt her.

Book two picks up as Essun works to master her powers. A plan is developing, one that could end the cataclysms striking the world, and she slowly grows more confident and in control. She begins to see some hope for the world, falls in love again, and takes on the role of protector. However, this is upended when her abilities unleash devastating consequences on the people she had grown close to, leaving her questioning her newfound conviction.

Finally, in book three, her arc reaches its peak. Essun discovers the location of her daughter, now many years since she was originally kidnapped. She's grown to be much like Essun was, bitter and angry and intent on using her abilities to end the world. This is a wakeup call for Essun, who rushes to her child's side to stop her, ultimately sacrificing herself and ending the cataclysms to prove that life is worth living. Though the trilogy ends on a sad note, it's clear just how much Essun has grown throughout her arc.

When compared to the *Jack Reacher* series, it's clear just how different these two stories are.

Unlike Essun, Jack is the protagonist of a static series, and doesn't change dramatically from book to book. He's a wandering vigilante, one who drifts through the U.S. (and sometimes abroad) after retiring from the U.S. Army. Through a series of odd jobs, he inevitably discovers some crime, mystery, or danger that becomes the focus of that book, and he's fairly consistent in his aggression and openness to violence.

Because of this, Jack doesn't have much of a character arc—though he does shape the arcs of those around him. Instead, the series iterates on the same basic setup in each book, and only occasionally brings up events and relationships from Jack's past.

Lessons from Chapter Seven

Ultimately, your main goal when writing series characters is consistency.

Even if your characters grow and change dramatically from book to book, you want that growth to feel natural. It needs to seem like a logical progression of their arc, or like a natural repeat of who they were in the previous books in the case of a static series.

This is especially important for your protagonist, but it applies to other characters too. The better you understand your cast, the easier it'll be to keep track of who they are throughout your series, so you can reflect that accurately in each subsequent book.

This is one reason why I encourage series authors to spend some extra time on their side characters. You have so much room to explore your cast that it seems like a waste not to give other characters their time in the sun. There's a practical side of this too. In many series, there might be long stretches of time between your protagonist's major turning points, time that could be filled by other arcs. Even if your hero doesn't face a big crossroad in book five, their closest ally might, making it easier to hold up the character side of your series without having to tie your story in knots.

Before we wrap up this chapter, I have one last piece of advice—and that's to think of your series as a life cycle.

As your series unfolds, your characters may be growing as people, but they might also be growing in terms of age. For each new season of life, how will the challenges they face evolve, and what new lessons will they need to learn?

Though simple, this can often unlock whole pillars of your series you never would have seen otherwise!

In the meantime, here are a few questions to help you apply what you've learned to your story:

- How will your series type shape your protagonist's internal journey?

- What belief holds your protagonist back throughout your series?
- What lesson do they need to learn or teach, and how will this change as your series unfolds?
- What about your protagonist will remain consistent in every book you write?

Once you've answered these questions, I'll see you in Chapter Eight!

8

TURNING BACK TIME

There are a handful of things in the writing world that consistently raise the ire of both authors and editors alike. Flashbacks, cliffhangers, and prologues are some of the biggest—but, in the context of this book, the one we really need to talk about is prequels.

Deep down, nothing on that list is objectively wrong, despite what internet forums and creative writing teachers might tell you. The stigma around them comes from how they're used. All of these require a lot of care and skill to do well, and for a series, nowhere is this more obvious than with prequels.

Prequels are inherently difficult to write, because by their very nature, readers already know how they're going to end. They've seen the future, and that makes it hard to create real, meaningful stakes for the story at hand.

No one was worried Han would die in *Solo*. We had all seen *A New Hope* decades ago!

And yet...

Just like my undying love of prologues (a conversation for a future book), prequels can be used to great effect. If nothing else, they give readers another taste of the world and characters they've come to love—and when done well, they can become an integral part of your larger fictional universe.

The question is, would a prequel fit the series you're creating? And, if so, how can you write one that won't feel like a foregone conclusion?

How to Write a Prequel

First things first—we need to talk about where prequels fit within the series types we've been discussing.

A prequel is simply a story set before the plot of your main series, focusing on past events that set the stage for your original books. Often, this comes in the form of a standalone novel, though plenty of authors create longer prequel series as well. This puts prequels almost in the realm of extended universes, and I find that's the easiest way to think of them. A prequel isn't "part" of your main series per se, but it does supplement it.

With that said, prequels introduce some complications above and beyond your usual extended universe. The premise of a typical prequel looks something like this:

How (character from the original series) got their (powers, abilities, fears, relationships, et cetera).

This is where things get tricky. Though this is a perfectly valid premise (one that could work if handled correctly), it also makes it oh so tempting to retread old ground. Because of this, many prequels have familiar flaws:

- The story has no stakes, because the end is already set in stone
- It rehashes your original novels, repeating the character arcs of the main series
- Or it outright negates the main series, swinging too far in the opposite direction

A good prequel honors the story it precedes, but also does its own thing—and that isn't easy to pull off.

Fortunately, "not easy" doesn't mean "impossible."

As a baseline, a prequel is no different than any other novel. It needs to stand on its own merit, and that means you need a strong core conflict, a compelling plot, steady pacing, and engaging characters.

PREQUEL SERIES STRUCTURE

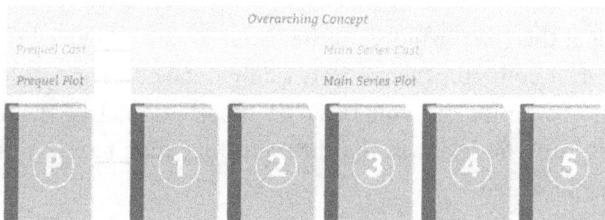

From there, you can start to consider how it links back to your main series. To capture readers' attention, your prequel needs to introduce something new, adding spice and life to a story that's otherwise already half-told. This is where the art of good prequels happens, and it's also where you'll want to remember five key things:

———

Always Honor the Original:

More than anything else, your prequel should pay respect to your original series.

This is good advice for any novel in a series, but it's particularly pertinent here. There's always the temptation to throw up your hands and tell whatever vaguely historical story you want, original series be damned (hello, *Fantastic Beasts*).

Realistically though, the readers buying your prequel are those who already loved your original series. They're coming back because they want to capture what those old novels made them feel. They want to soak up that world again, and relive the magic as much as possible.

Because of this, you need to know what drew readers into your series in the first place.

Was it the vibe or mood of the story? Was it a beloved character, a powerful theme, or a richly detailed magic system? What promise did you make in those original books, and how can you leverage that heart to fuel your prequel, or at least inform it?

This is why it's so disappointing when a prequel invalidates chunks of your main series. Readers aren't here for a retcon —they're here for more of what they already love.

Write Something Substantial:

Of course, to be worth reading, your prequel needs depth.

This is why I said good prequels follow all the same rules as any other novel. They need to be a fully developed story, complete with meaningful conflicts and plots, rather than something you could have told in a flashback—and you definitely don't want to just rehash the same character arcs and conflicts as before.

Because of this, don't be afraid to look farther afield when brainstorming a prequel. Any past events that were implied but never explored are fair game!

Here are a few ideas you could play with:

- How did your magic system/technology come to be?
- How did your protagonist become a spy/teacher/astronaut/chef?
- How did the dystopia in your main series start?
- How did the feud between tribes/characters/countries begin?
- How did dragons/unicorns/giants/robots go extinct?
- How did the mob/raiders/ruling party gain power?
- How did that character end up lost in the woods?

Though "my protagonist, but younger" is a valid foundation for a prequel, I hope this shows the variety on offer. You can absolutely write a fantastic prequel with a blank-slate hero. Oftentimes, that's actually the easier option.

Focus on How, Not What:

One thing you hopefully noticed in those examples was that every option started the same way. This was on purpose.

Rather than asking "what" happens, your prequel should ask "how."

Let's be real. Readers already know your characters survive (or die, depending on your original series) at the end of your prequel. The fact that it happens isn't all that interesting, but *how it happens* might be. This is where you can really lean into the puzzle of your prequel. What do readers already know, and how could you turn that on its head, revealing just how complex the past actually is?

A great example of this is *X-Men: First Class*.

This prequel sets up the rivalry between the main series' protagonist and antagonist, Charles Xavier and Erik Lehnsherr. We know they'll eventually become enemies, but at the outset, they look like true friends. It almost tricks us into believing their story might end differently, and it keeps us glued to the screen wondering how it'll all fall apart.

Though readers might know the ending, they won't know how you'll get there.

This is also why prequels tend to be more personal in nature. We know the world won't end at the end of your prequel (we need it to stick around for your main series), but that doesn't mean there aren't real stakes for your cast. Their relationships, experiences, wounds, and abilities are all things you can threaten or challenge, providing a lot of flexibility even if your plot is limited by your original series.

Add Some Fan Service:

Next, this is small, but something to consider nonetheless.

When readers dive into your prequel, they should see hints of your original series sprinkled throughout.

Again, readers are looking to recapture the magic of that main series, and small acts of fan service are a great way to provide that. Anything from a secret symbol to a mysterious artifact from your original story could work, as could character names, side stories, et cetera. Sometimes, you'll be expanding on things you only mentioned originally, but other times, you can just give a passing glance to things you touched on in the main series.

So long as it "pings" the part of your reader's brain that recognizes the familiar, it has the power to truly delight them, while also creating another link between your prequel and original series.

Give Yourself Space:

Last but not least, don't be afraid to give yourself space.

If you're struggling to write a prequel, sometimes you need to step back further in time. Your prequel doesn't need to be an immediate precursor to your main series. It could happen hundreds of years in the past or to an entirely separate cast of characters—the trick is, once again, to honor what readers loved about your original series.

Find that link, and then build a riveting story around it, even if it's far in the past.

———

With all that said, there's still a question we need to address: When would you really want to write a prequel?

Personally, I think prequels are pretty fun to write, but there are strategic reasons to consider them. A prequel might be part of your larger plan for your series (perhaps as a reader magnet or permafree first-in-series, which we'll chat about more in Chapter Thirteen), or you may just have a lot of history you're excited to explore.

However, it might also be that your series takes off!

If readers are clamoring for another book after you've "finished" your series, it may be worthwhile to consider a prequel. That gives you an easy way to expand the original story, without having to retcon past books to force a larger story. This is a bigger concern for sequential and episodic series, but even the other series types could benefit from a good prequel.

And finally, sometimes you'll want to write a series, but your story just isn't cooperating. We'll get into how to turn a standalone novel into a series later in this book, but for now, prequels are one of the easiest ways to create a series. A standalone novel plus a prequel is a solid duology—and though it isn't a long series by any means, it can still bring a lot of the benefits you might be looking for.

Lessons From Chapter Eight

Much like extended universes, prequels are a kind of weird part of the series world. But, they're also a tremendously fun one! A good prequel gives you lots of space to explore other sides of your story, and also gives you a simple way to return to your series in the future if you so desire.

The trick is thinking deeply about what readers are craving from your prequel. Like any other part of your series, you want to spend some time planning, ideating, and plotting out your prequel. Find secrets you can reveal, silly fan service to include, and a strong link back to your main series, and this becomes an awesome tool for your writing toolkit!

In the meantime, here are a few questions to help you apply what you've learned to your story:

- Would a prequel fit your goals for your series?
- What past events did you touch on in your main series, but didn't fully explore?
- Are there any past characters, events, or turning points you're excited about?
- How far back in time can you go while still maintaining a link to your original books?

Once you've answered these questions, I'll see you in Chapter Nine!

9

HOW TO WRITE A TRILOGY

I promised you a section on trilogies back in Chapter Six, and it's high time I made good on that promise!

Humans love sets of three. There's bound to be some psychological reason for this, but honestly, I don't know what it is. All I know is that three is a satisfying number, and nowhere is that more true than in the world of trilogies.

Trilogies are titans of the fiction-writing world. Authors love them because they give us enough space to explore complex stories without getting overwhelmed, and writing one is generally seen as a big accomplishment. Meanwhile, a good trilogy provides something substantial for readers to sink their teeth into, but isn't the same kind of yearslong commitment as a longer series. No matter what side of the equation you're on, trilogies are consistently (and understandably) beloved.

So, let's take a moment to look at why trilogies work so well.

Why Trilogies Work

Trilogies are a fascinating subject, precisely because of how popular they are.

For many authors, a sequential trilogy is the gold standard of fictional series, but that's not just because they sell well. Because trilogies have dominated the series space for so long, they've started to develop something of their own pattern. A well-written trilogy has its own cadence and rhythm, in many ways unique from other types of series.

Here's a quick look at what this rhythm looks like:

- **Book One:** The story begins! Here the author sets expectations for the series, introduces the premise of the story, and ends on an exciting finale that turns out to be just one piece of a much larger puzzle.
- **Book Two:** The story grows deeper. New secrets are revealed, and it turns out the core conflict is more complex than we realized. This book ends on a low note, where our heroes face a painful defeat that calls their future into question.
- **Book Three:** The conclusion of the story. This ends the series' overarching plot, tying together the threads set up in prior books. The characters face their steepest challenge yet, complete their arcs, and finally rest. We breathe a sigh of relief as we look at what life will be like now that the journey is over— often calling back to the beginning of book one.

This pattern is definitely rooted in story structure, like any good series. If you look close enough, you might even recognize some points from our earlier discussion of plot! But it's also something of its own thing. Regardless of the structure an author prefers, from the Four Act Structure to the Hero's Journey, most successful trilogies will mimic this rhythm.

As you might imagine, this presents some unique benefits, but also some potential pitfalls.

The biggest danger when writing a trilogy is what's called the "book two low," where the story settles into a slump that readers never get out of. Book two is often the longest by a decent margin, and is all about the characters slowly coming to grips with their new world, abilities, and challenges.

That can definitely be riveting, but it can also become a slog. Book two has to bridge the gap between books one and three, without the benefits of either. Book one is fresh and exciting, and book three puts us on a crash course with the series finale. Meanwhile, book two just needs to move us forward, setting up the dominoes we'll eventually push over later in the series.

Because of this, the second book in a trilogy lives or dies by how it raises the stakes:

- New characters may arrive and old ones leave, changing the dynamic of the story.
- We might shift to new locations, or reveal secrets and surprises about past ones.
- Things your reader took for granted in book one may not be as simple as they seemed.
- Past relationships could resurface, bringing old wounds with them.
- And the mechanics or rules of your world might become deeper and more complex.

A trilogy like *The Lord of the Rings* does this well.

In the second book, the cast splinters off into three groups, each heading off on different paths rife with their own challenges. This creates multiple pockets of adventure, making space for a variety of characters new and old to take center stage. The stakes increase as our trust in different characters is threatened, and the balance of power is always shifting—creating a story that's anything but boring.

Of course, this isn't the only danger when writing a trilogy. There is one other pitfall many authors fall into, and that's the tendency to write themselves into a corner. In an attempt to make book two interesting, it's easy to raise the stakes so high that you don't know how to save your characters by the end of book three. Instead, you end up relying on too-convenient solutions or plot contrivances to resolve the story, and readers leave deflated. After all, they were excited to see all the clever ways you planned to resolve the story.

Because of this, trilogies (like most series) do best with a bit of forward planning.

You always want one eye on your finale, and at least some idea of how your characters will get themselves out of trouble. With that to ground you, it becomes much easier to keep the story engaging, *without* causing headaches later on down the line.

Case Study: Star Wars

To help you see this rhythm at work, I want to point to *Star Wars*. This is a wide-ranging extended universe, with some amazing entries and some less amazing ones. However, one thing they've consistently gotten right is the structure of their trilogies.

Take the original trilogy:

- **A New Hope:** Luke's life is upended by the arrival of two droids, and he sets out on an adventure across the galaxy. Along the way, he gets pulled into the Rebel Alliance, awakens to the Force, and destroys the Death Star—but the battle is far from won, and his previously simple journey to save a princess is now far more complex.

- **The Empire Strikes Back:** Luke and the Rebel Alliance continue their fight against the Empire, enlisting new allies to help their cause. Meanwhile, Luke struggles to harness the Force, raising the stakes of the story. We end on a low note. Luke's true parentage is revealed, shattering his beliefs about who he is. The story ends with us uncertain about how our heroes will recover.

- **Return of the Jedi:** After regrouping, Luke and the Rebel Alliance stage their biggest attack yet. But rather than fall back into old routines, Luke takes a new route. He surrenders himself to the Empire and faces his father, tapping into his humanity and saving the Rebels. The Empire is defeated, and we rest easy as we watch the characters we've come to love finally at peace.

This is basically a textbook example of the trilogy structure we just discussed—but what's extra interesting is how it mirrors many of the other examples from this book. From the *Broken Earth* trilogy in Chapter Seven to *The Hunger Games*, I encourage you to look back on all the trilogies we've covered to find this rhythm.

You might be surprised by just how consistent it really is!

Lessons from Chapter Nine

To recap, here's what I hope you take away from this chapter:

- Trilogies have a unique rhythm. This is either comforting or limiting, depending on your mindset.
- Always write with the end in mind, to avoid backing yourself into a corner.
- Beware the book two low! This is often the hardest book to write, so find creative ways to raise the stakes and add new dynamics to your story.
- And know the stories that came before you—even if you plan to chart your own path.

Trilogies are a blast to write, and something I personally love to experiment with. However, as fun as they are, don't feel like they're your only option. They're popular for sure, but other lengths of series have their place. Duologies are rapidly gaining ground (and even developing their own unique cadence), and trilogies are best suited for sequential-style series anyways. Static and anthology trilogies do exist, but they're definitely on the rare side.

Rather than being the "one true way" to write a series, I hope this becomes just another tool in your writing arsenal!

In the meantime, here are a few questions to help you apply what you've learned to your story:

- How does your series mimic the three-part trilogy structure we discussed?
- Does book two raise the stakes in engaging ways?
- How will you get your characters out of trouble, without it feeling contrived?

- What trilogies can you look towards for inspiration as you craft your own?

Once you've answered these questions, I'll see you in Part Three!

III

BUILDING YOUR FICTIONAL SERIES

"It's such a confidence trick, writing a novel. The main person you have to trick into confidence is yourself."

ZADIE SMITH

10

PLAN, EXPAND, REVIVE

As we shift our focus away from theory and into the practical matters of writing a series, I want to start with a quick story about the origins of this book.

I've been debating what to name this chapter for a while now, and as I write this intro, I'm pretty much out of time. This book is due to my beta readers in just a few hours, so I'm literally typing this before hitting export and sending it away. I used to have an awesome name in mind (one that fit so perfectly that it was the inspiration for this entire book), but in the end, I stole that name for something else.

In my original draft, this was called "Beyond Book One!"

Yep. When it came down to it, I demoted poor Chapter Ten and ended up using that title on a larger scale. No set of words better captures the inspiration behind *Beyond Book One*—and though it might not look like it now, this chapter was actually the first chapter I ever planned when working on this idea.

You see, deep in my soul, I'm a standalone writer.

When a new novel comes to me, it almost always does so as a single, self-contained story. I try to stretch it into a longer series, but more often than not, the whole process feels forced. I've been fighting against this since the earliest days of my writing career, and in the beginning, I was convinced it meant I could never succeed as an author. Like so many of us, I was used to hearing that authors had to publish in a series to make a living. Readers expected it. The algorithm favored it. And yet, I just couldn't seem to do it.

Fortunately, if you've ever met me, you'll know that I'm stubborn to a fault. As far as I'm concerned, any problem is a puzzle that can be solved, and how to expand a story "beyond book one" has been my puzzle of choice for some time now.

Though it eventually expanded into the world of series structure and extended universes, that was the real origin of everything you've read so far: How you (and I) can take the ideas in our heads and turn them into functional, successful series, without feeling like we're forcing our novels through some kind of Play-Doh spaghetti press.

So, whether you're starting from scratch, building from an existing story, or reviving a dormant series, this chapter is where your ideas will finally start coming together!

Starting a Series From Scratch

To kick things off, let's begin with the easiest way to craft a series—planning one from the ground up.

When writing a series, having a plan is especially important, regardless of how you usually prefer to write. You have a lot to juggle if you want your series to make sense, so knowing the basics *before* you start will save you a lot of misery later.

How far you expand this plan from there will be up to you, but even pantsers can benefit from a loose map of their series.

Ideally, this process begins with your overarching concept. You hopefully decided on your series type back in Chapter Five, and maybe even got some ideas for how your story could unfold. Now you need to put that inspiration into concrete terms. Will you be focused on an overarching plot, an overarching character, or an overarching setup, theme, or world? How will that concept take shape, and how could you summarize it in just one sentence?

Depending on your series type, your focus will be a bit different:

- **Sequential Series:** What is the core conflict driving your series? How does this conflict shape your characters and world, how does it create stakes, and how will it be resolved in the end?
- **Episodic Series:** Same as above, but with room for more. Alongside those questions, what smaller side stories could supplement (but still connect to) this core conflict?
- **Static Series:** Who is your protagonist throughout the series? What are their defining traits, and how will readers identify with and relate to them? What repeating conflicts, situations, or challenges will they face throughout the series, and why?
- **Anthology Series:** What common setup, theme, or world will ground your series? How can you iterate on that idea in interesting ways, while still maintaining some connection to that original concept?

The clearer you are here, the stronger your series' foundation will be.

From there, work on expanding your overarching concept into a short premise. This is the elevator pitch for your series, and is a simple, one or two-sentence synopsis of your big idea. An easy formula for this premise is:

A character wants something, works to reach that goal, faces conflict and obstacles, and thus changes or creates change in the world around them.

Again, static and anthology series will change this format slightly—but the same general setup still applies. Static series will talk about the common types of conflicts (rather than a specific one), while anthology series will center on a type of character (rather than a named protagonist).

With your premise in hand, spend an hour or two brain dumping any and all ideas you have related to your series. These don't need to be in any logical order, or even strictly "good" ideas. This phase is simply an invitation for your muse to come out and play. Once you have a substantial brain dump completed, you can start parsing through it and looking for themes. How could you organize these ideas into individual books? How could they take shape as smaller, book-specific plots and conflicts? And which ideas are most exciting to you, and thus the ones that should shape your series the most?

Your end goal after all this work is to have created a short summary for each book in your series (or a small handful, if you're writing an ongoing static or anthology series). Depending on your writing style, these could be just a few sentences, but they could also take shape as larger outlines if you so choose.

Either way, this forms your baseline.

In these notes, you now have the broad shape of your series —both to help you puzzle through all the gaps you might face, and to keep you from writing yourself into a corner later. This is what you'll share when friends and readers ask what's next for your series, and it's what will keep you focused on the light ahead when you're lost in the weeds and your series feels like a tangled mess.

Keep this plan close, because it'll be a vital asset as you charge ahead!

From Standalone to Series

Of course, true to the name of this book, we also need to chat about reverse engineering a series.

If you've already written a standalone novel (or planned a standalone you want to expand on), you have a slightly harder road ahead of you. But, it's far from an impossible one. Much like before, our goal here is simply to get your bearings, giving your creative brain a logical path to follow as you puzzle through all the ways you could stretch your story.

First up, we need to figure out what you already have:

- Where did you end the last book?
- What arcs did you complete or leave open-ended?
- What points of view is the story told from?
- What exactly is the core conflict of this book?
- What message or theme are you focused on?

- How fleshed out is your story's world?

Take some notes based on these questions, and then think about the expectations you've already set. What do your readers expect will carry through into the rest of the series, both in terms of your conflict, cast, and tone, but also style, pacing, and emotions? What questions did you leave unanswered in that first book, even if they're small? What was your larger vision for the story, and how could you continue that vision in new ways?

This will hopefully spark some ideas, specifically in terms of the type of series you want to write. Different series mesh with different stories, so the type you choose will play a big role in where your novels go from here:

- **Sequential Series:** Your biggest concern here is how you can expand your core conflict into a larger overarching plot. Was there a deeper conflict brewing beneath the surface of this story? And if so, how could you draw that conflict out?
- **Episodic Series:** Similar to sequential series, your focus should be on your core conflict. However, you'll also want to consider whether book one fits the episodic mold. Is it short and focused enough to act as a stepping stone into an episodic series?
- **Static Series:** Who is your protagonist in book one, and how could you put them into a similar but different situation in future books? What challenges could you throw their way that would be unique and interesting, but thematically connected? This is often the easiest way to expand an existing novel.
- **Anthology Series:** For an anthology series, the sky's the limit! Could you tell alternate stories set

elsewhere in your world? Could you repeat a common theme or setup? What new characters could you put in similar situations, and what new points of view could you focus on? Side characters are a boon here, but make sure you're crystal clear on the overarching concept of this new series.

Really, the secret to doing this well is being careful to respect your original story.

You obviously can't abandon the decisions you made in that first novel, even if they dug you into a hole long term. If that's the case, don't panic. It may take more time, but there are very few stories that have truly hit a dead end. Instead, give yourself space to explore new possibilities, keeping a few key things in mind:

———

Honor Your Natural Structure:

Every novel has a structure that suits it. The sprawling, epic nature of the *Broken Earth* trilogy is a perfect fit for a sequential series, while the cozy vibe of the twenty-nine entry *The Cat Who...* mysteries feels natural as a static series.

Whatever your novel is about, aim to pick a series type that highlights its strengths.

World First, Story Second:

If you're unsure how to expand your story, stop focusing on the story itself—focus on your world instead! What side characters could you explore or develop? What new locations, relationships, mysteries, or mechanics could you introduce? Could you have an entirely new protagonist in the next book, or elevate a subplot you only hinted at originally? Did you name any characters, places, or events, but never explain them?

Any small detail could be the open window you need to spark a sequel, and a whole new set of stories you otherwise would have missed.

Aim to Add Value:

One of the biggest traps authors fall into when expanding a story is adding fluff just for the sake of doing so.

Don't get me wrong—this is tricky to manage, especially considering the advice I just gave you. However, anything you add to your series needs to *mean* something. It needs to have a purpose in your larger narrative and link back to that overarching concept I'm constantly going on about. So, before charging ahead, take some time to think about how those changes would add to (rather than overwhelm) the real heart of your series.

Know Your Promise:

Building off the previous point, it helps to know what you promised readers in your first novel. Are you creating a childish, playful story, or an intense, gritty adventure? Your series' tone makes all the other elements we've discussed come together, so be cautious as you expand your series.

Readers want to recapture the magic they felt in that first book. So, just like you want to honor your series' natural structure, you also want to honor the promise you made in your original story.

Avoid the Dreaded Retcon:

One of the biggest mistakes I see authors make is going for the easy out when their series gets messy—specifically by undoing past character development just to write a sequel.

If your protagonist experienced a major arc in your original novel, *and* they'll still be your protagonist in the next book, you have to account for that in the sequel. Scrapping their old journey and rehashing it in a new way isn't satisfying, and will quickly have readers leaving for a different story.

There's nothing wrong with playing with expectations, upending what readers assumed was true, and even taking away plot armor that used to shield your characters. Just do so in a way that respects the developments of past books.

Don't Be Precious:

Last but not least, don't be afraid to stay flexible when writing your series.

This is a painful piece of advice, and one I often have to give myself too. As authors, we *adore* our novels. They're vibrant and real in our minds, and that makes it easy to forget that there's no "one way" for that story to exist. Struggling with your protagonist? Change your point of view in the second book! Stuck on a mechanic you can't figure out? Reveal a surprising twist for the rest of the series!

Obviously, you don't want to trick readers here—but really, this is about us, not them. Our stories aren't precious, and if clinging to some frustrating idea is the difference between writing your series or scrapping it, I'll always vote that you try something new. Know what pieces you refuse to compromise. But, for everything else, give yourself space to experiment in service of the larger story.

———

Like it or not, writing a series based on an existing novel will always take you longer than if you were starting from scratch. This is a tricky process, and you're bound to face some writer's block at least once along the way.

However, there are always options.

For example, say you've written a standalone fantasy novel that comes to a nice, clean conclusion at the end. That might be pretty hard to expand on—but, what if you wrote a prequel based on an old wives' tale told in that first book? That would form a duology, and while that isn't a long series by any means, it is one way you can expand your story into an anthology series.

That's basically what the original *The Graceling Realm* trilogy did. The first book was a standalone, but was then expanded with a book two prequel, and later a book three sequel. Though the author has expanded the series since then, it just goes to show that your series doesn't have to be complicated to succeed.

Waking Up a Dormant Series

Finally, what if you already have an ongoing series, and are simply trying to inject some new life into it?

Well (and I'm sure you're sick of me saying this), this will once again depend on the type of series you're writing. There are two basic paths here:

- **Sequential/Episodic:** If you're writing a sequential or episodic series, you hopefully have some sort of finale in mind—but if not, that should be your first order of business. How will you wrap up this series in a way that's satisfying to readers, resolving the core conflict of your plot and tying off any character arcs you've created?

- **Static/Anthology:** Static and anthology series are more flexible, but you still need an overarching concept to guide you. Drill down to this concept and get clear on what exactly you're promising readers in each book. Then, look at the common themes, patterns, or setups you've focused on thus far. How could you define those in simple terms?

Once that foundation is in place, you can start gathering ideas and repeating the process we've already discussed throughout this chapter. Again, this is the time to tempt your muse, turn on your magpie brain, and collect everything you can. Movies, music, art, long walks in the forest...

Anything is fair game if it gets you inspired!

Lessons from Chapter Ten

Writing a series can be a frustrating endeavor—whether you're working from scratch or building from something you've already written.

It's likely you'll feel frustrated or unsure at various points in the process, and when that happens, I want you to pause. What's the big picture here? What story are you really itching to tell? That should be your guiding star throughout this endeavor. So long as you know the vision you're working towards, everything else will fall into place.

In the meantime, here are a few questions to help you apply what you've learned to your story:

- What state is your series currently in?

- How can you turn your overarching concept into smaller, individual books?
- What are your reader's expectations, and how will you honor those?
- And where could you go for inspiration and ideas to rejuvenate your series?

Once you've answered these questions, I'll see you in Chapter Eleven!

11

THE ALL-IMPORTANT SERIES BIBLE

A s a good friend of mine often says, some people are just worksheet people—and for authors, I'd say most of us are.

Working out your story on paper helps you get your ideas out of your head and into a concrete form. Our brains are often so jumbled with notes, characters, plot threads, and to-do lists that seeing our ideas physically in front of us is one of the best ways to cut through the noise. Even if you're not filling out a literal worksheet, writing down the facts for your series can be immensely clarifying.

And that's where a series bible comes in!

A series bible is a short, five or six-page document that covers the most important information about your series. This includes things like your overarching concept and characters, but also your genre, your series promise, and a basic timeline of key events. This is similar to an outline, though I would consider them separate things. While an outline is an exhaustive map of your story, a series bible is more "at-a-glance," giving you a thirty-thousand-foot view of your series to help you write and plan each entry.

This is fantastic for keeping details consistent from book to book—and it also reduces the amount of time you'll spend flipping through past novels trying to remember names, places, or facts. Depending on how long your series is, you could have substantial downtime between writing your first book and your last. By creating a series bible, you give yourself an easier way to bridge that gap and jump back into the series after time away.

So, in the spirit of worksheets, here's how to start a series bible of your own!

Building Your Series Bible

By now, you should have everything you need to fill out this template, so this should be a fairly quick chapter. We've discussed all of these topics throughout this book—meaning now, it's just a matter of grabbing a pen and committing your ideas to paper (if you haven't already).

There are twelve sections to include in your series bible:

———

Your Series Type:

First, write down the type of series you're creating, whether sequential, episodic, static, or anthology.

Genre/Subgenre:

What genre are you writing in? List four or five conventions of that genre that you'll need to be aware of while writing your series. These are the things readers expect based on other popular stories in your niche. If you're not sure where to start with this, I recommend looking to both classics in your genre and recent bestsellers for inspiration.

Length:

How long will each book in your series be? Give a range here, like sixty to eighty thousand words, or thirty to fifty thousand words. This will be shaped by your series type and genre—but it's also not a hard rule. Instead, use this as a rough metric when writing each entry, even if you end up slightly outside your target range.

Overarching Concept:

We're back again! I'm sure you're tired of hearing about this, but take some time to summarize your overarching concept in a single sentence, or record the concept you created earlier in this book. The clearer this concept is, the stronger your series' foundation will be (otherwise I wouldn't keep harping on it).

Book Cards:

Next up, it's time to shift our attention to the individual entries of your series.

There are two ways to handle this, depending on your style. You can either list each entry in a larger document, or you can create what I like to call "book cards." These are simply index cards with the title or working title of each novel, alongside a few key details you'll need to keep things organized.

No matter which option you prefer, use this as a chance to write down every book in your series (if you're writing a sequential or episodic series) or as many books as you have planned (for static and anthology series). Then, describe the premise of each novel in a short paragraph.

Plot Points:

If you're using index cards, now it's time to flip them over and add some details!

Alongside your book summaries, you'll also want to note how that book connects to your overarching concept. For a sequential or episodic series, where does it fall in the Four Act Structure? Does it include any of the crossroads we discussed, or any other plot point you need to keep track of? For static and anthology series, simply describe how this story links back to and builds on the overarching concept of the whole series

Series Timeline:

Based on your new book cards, make a brief timeline of the key events in your series. These are things like character introductions, deaths, major changes in relationships or abilities, and other key moments that will affect and shape later entries.

For example, in the first book of *The Hunger Games*, we get hints of some place called District 13. However, we don't actually see the district until much later. Knowing what foreshadowing you need to pay off throughout your series will make it much easier to write each book.

Character Profiles:

Similar to your timeline, I also recommend creating some simple character profiles. Focus on major, repeat characters here, like your protagonist, key allies, and possibly villains. How do they change from book to book, and what milestones do they hit throughout your series? What details will you need to keep consistent?

Locations, Mechanics, and Rules:

This process repeats again for your worldbuilding. Like before, write a short paragraph describing any important settings, technology, magic, or other rules that will play a major role in your series.

If you're writing a static or anthology series that lacks consistent locations, instead note the kinds of places you want to explore. What common elements do they share, and how does this all work as a cohesive world?

Tone and Mood:

What is the primary emotion underpinning your series? Will these stories be melancholy and moody, or light and upbeat? What's the point of this series, and what kind of experience are you promising your readers?

Your Goals for the Series:

What are your goals for this series? These could be publishing related (like releasing the full set within two years) or personal (like winning a local fiction award). Whatever goals you choose, try to make them clear, specific, and measurable. This way, you can reflect back and see the progress you've made in concrete terms.

Your Style Guide:

Last but not least, I'd also recommend a short style guide.

This final section is optional, so feel free to skip it if needed. However, if you do want to create one, this is simply a list of spellings, proper names, punctuation rules, formatting preferences, et cetera. If you handed your manuscript to a proofreader, what aspects of your writing style would they need to know to keep your draft consistent? Do you italicize internal monologues, or put them in quotes? Is that character's name spelled Coruscar or Corsucar?

You might be surprised how much hand-wringing this could save you down the line!

———

This probably looks like a lot, but ideally, your finished series bible will only be a few pages long. None of these items need to be exhaustively detailed—they just need to be something you can ground yourself with as you charge forward into writing.

Of course, this is also just one way to build a series bible.

Some authors use their series bible the way I would use an outline, creating huge, deep documents exploring every detail of their series. Others focus on things I didn't include, or scrap items I feel are important. Either way, think of this template as a starting place. You're welcome to adapt it as you need to fit your personal style.

Lessons from Chapter Eleven

As one final note, I encourage you to think of your series bible as a living document—not as something set in stone.

When writing your series, some things are bound to change. No matter how detailed of a planner you might be, there are certain things you'll only learn by writing your first draft. Characters gain a mind of their own, events get shuffled around, and new mechanics are introduced. Your series bible isn't here to limit you, but to provide a record of how your series is developing.

So, don't be afraid to add notes, scribble in the margins, or even cut your series bible up and paste it into a scrapbook. The sky's the limit, so long as it's helping you bring your series to life!

In the meantime, here are a few questions to help you apply what you've learned to your story:

- Do you have a clear set of notes outlining the key details of your series?
- How could you organize your ideas so they're easy to reference later?

Once you've answered these questions, I'll see you in Chapter Twelve!

12

MANAGING THE WRITING PROCESS

W e've covered a lot of ground throughout this book, but up until now, we've mostly been focused on planning rather than writing. That was an important step to ensure you had a steady foundation to build your series from, but in this chapter, that needs to change—starting with a question:

What's your risk tolerance?

I ask because everyone's openness to risk is a bit different. Personally, I'm game for almost anything. I'll go skydiving, eat strange foods I can neither pronounce nor recognize, and leap into new projects even when I'm terrified they'll go horribly wrong. However, I also don't take risks needlessly. I look to the people around me for advice, weigh my options before making a decision, and get a sense of what the worst case would actually be if I made the wrong choice.

The key to this is finding a balance that works for you. Some would say I'm way too risky. Others would think I'm a shut-in. And many people would believe all of us are crazy! After all, writing and publishing novels is a risk in and of itself, one lots of aspiring authors never actually take.

Fortunately, you've made it this far—and though there are definitely risks ahead, there are just as many clever ways to write a successful series.

How to Write a Series

As the beginning of this chapter alluded to, how you choose to write your series is really about how you manage risk. Some authors are happy to write their whole series in one go, potentially spending years of their life on a mostly unproven story. Others prefer to publish each book as it's finished, thus accepting a completely different set of risks.

There are two sides to this:

- The risk of wasting time on a series that doesn't work
- Or the risk of backing yourself into a corner with a series that does

Depending on the writing method you choose, you'll face a blend of these risks. There's no way to eliminate them entirely, but there are ways to mitigate them, allowing you to find a balance that suits you.

———

Writing All At Once:

First up, many authors choose to write their entire series before publishing—basically like one, gigantic novel. With this style, it'll be a long time before you're ready to share your series, but it also reduces the risk of locking yourself on a path you later hate. It's easy to fix plot holes, revise earlier books, and ensure your series feels like a solid unit, even if it requires some delayed gratification.

Of course, the flip side is that this increases the risk to your time. Writing your series all in one go is a gamble, and it makes it harder for you to adapt based on reader feedback, trends in your genre, or your own changing preferences. Plus, you may never even get that far. Plenty of authors burn out halfway through writing with this method. They just get sick of their story.

Because of that, this is generally best for short sequential (and sometimes episodic) series. If you're writing a duology or a trilogy, crafting the entire story at once becomes a lot more manageable, and the benefits start to outweigh the drawbacks.

Batching Books:

In contrast, batching your books is a great option for basically any type of series—static, anthology, the works.

With this option, you commit to writing two or three novels in one go, and then publish them while you work on the next batch. This helps you maintain a steady release schedule, but also gives you space to rest, experiment with other stories, and adjust your plans based on how your series is received. It takes a bit of stamina, but it isn't quite as intense as building your entire series in one go.

Honestly, that makes this my preferred middle ground. By batching your books, you make it easier to revise and polish your series, but you also get feedback faster. Though you'll be taking on a bit of both risks, neither is out of control, and that makes this an especially good option for longer series or those with no defined end.

Writing One at a Time:

Finally, we have both the easiest and riskiest option (if you can call writing a novel "easy").

Here, you write each entry of your series much like you would a standalone novel. You plan, draft, and revise it, press publish, and only then move on to the next. With this method, you only have to commit to one book at a time, and that gives you a much easier way out if your series doesn't go the way you expected. Though we all hope our series turns out perfectly, life is complicated—sometimes your situation means you need to step back from a story you otherwise loved.

Unfortunately, this opens you up to a lot of other risks. By writing only one novel at a time, it can be harder to maintain a steady release schedule. Unexpected edits and roadblocks will happen, and that can lead to lulls between entries. This is perhaps the biggest flaw of this method. When you leave big gaps between books, readers are much more likely to move on, or refuse to start your series entirely. Far too many series are left unfinished by their authors. Readers who have been burnt by this in the past often won't touch a series until they know it's complete.

You'll also need a solid plan to pull this off. Once a book is published, it becomes much harder to go back and update things based on newer books. To avoid writing yourself into a corner, a robust outline is more important than ever.

———

Which of these paths is right for you will depend on a lot of factors—from your series type to the length of each book, your genre, and your personal writing style. If you're writing a short series of romance novellas, batching a few books or even writing as you go is a less intimidating option. But, if you're trying to pull off a complex, twelve-book epic fantasy, that prospect becomes much harder.

All three of these methods have their place, and you may dabble with all of them at different points in your writing career.

For now though, I would start by considering your risk tolerance. There's a reason I opened this chapter with that question! The longer you take to write your series, the more time you could have spent building a readership and seizing new opportunities. But the faster you move and the more you batch, the more you risk spending all that time on a series you're ultimately unhappy with.

Though I certainly hope that last situation doesn't happen to you (and this book should help mitigate that), it's still a risk worth considering.

Making Your Series Sustainable

Once you've decided how you'll write your series, all that's left is the practical matter of actually doing so.

This is a long process, no matter how you approach it. Writing a series takes stamina, patience, self-care, and a whole lot of work. Developing healthy writing habits is critical to reaching "The End," so there are a few points to keep in mind as you move forward:

- Don't overwork yourself—aim to strike a balance between progress and rest.
- Beware of burnout, and give your mind breaks when it asks for them.
- Write consistently, whether that's the same time every Saturday or every morning before work.
- Find a support system to lean on, encourage you, and keep you grounded.
- Mix things up when your series gets stale! It's ok to have side projects and other hobbies to keep your brain refreshed.
- Avoid shiny object syndrome. It's ok to dabble with other stories, but the only way to finish your series is to stay focused as much as possible.

Alongside these general best practices, I'd also recommend keeping a progress log.

Your mindset will naturally fluctuate throughout the writing process. Perhaps you get stuck thirty thousand words into every novel you write, or maybe your Third Crossroad always triggers a mental block. You might struggle to write during the summer when kids are home, or you may deal with seasonal depression, making December a slow month for your series.

Though this might sound weird, our brains are surprisingly consistent. And by keeping a log of your writing, it'll be much easier to notice patterns in your creativity and prepare for the slumps you'll face in future books.

What this progress log looks like is up to you—it's really just a journal for your writing! Here's what I include in my log, to give you a starting point:

- The date of each writing session
- What part of the story I'm working on
- How many words I wrote
- How long I took to write them
- How I'm feeling at the end of the session
- And what's going on in my life, both good and bad

Last but not least, know that you'll face a lot of pressure as a series author—and that's ok.

There's something both addictive and terrifying about knowing hundreds of readers are waiting for your next novel. It's intense, and it often creates something called the "second-book slump." With this, authors feel so paralyzed by the need to "live up to" their first book that writing their second becomes nearly impossible.

This makes a lot of sense, but it's really just your mind playing tricks on you. If you start to feel overwhelmed by this pressure, remember that readers enjoyed your first novel for a reason. Take some time to step back from your series and figure out what that reason was. Honor it, and then give yourself permission to trust your past self. If you've been following along with this book, you should have at least some plan for how your series will unfold. It's ok to follow that plan, knowing your series will come together by the time it's all through.

Above all, this is *your* story.

Learning from feedback is great, but ultimately, you're the captain of this ship. We'll talk more about this in Chapter Fourteen, but for now, don't be afraid to pursue your vision full steam ahead!

Lessons from Chapter Twelve

With all that said, these techniques and tactics are great—but the truth is, sometimes your series will just surprise you. It'll change over time, upend even the best of plans, and challenge you to remain flexible even when you're feeling stiff and tired. As you write, you'll discover new things about your story, and that's ok.

Even if you intended to write your series one way or the other, don't be afraid to adapt when the situation calls for it. The work you've done up until now will always be there to guide you forward, even when your writing takes a new turn.

In the meantime, here are a few questions to help you apply what you've learned to your story:

- What risks are you willing (or unwilling) to take when writing your series?
- Would you prefer to risk time spent writing, or risk locking yourself into a story you're unhappy with?
- How will you care for your mental well-being while writing your series?

Once you've answered these questions, I'll see you in Chapter Thirteen!

13

PUBLISHING A SUCCESSFUL SERIES

There's always a risk when writing chapters like these that things go out of date, sometimes before the book is even released. Sales trends, algorithms, technology, and techniques are always evolving, and honestly, the best way to learn is often by watching the authors around you.

Still, there are some things that have held fast over the years, and that have played a big role in why series are such a boon for indie authors. Many publishing strategies only really work when you have multiple connected novels to play with —and even things like pricing and preorders are a bit different for series than for standalone novels.

Though this chapter won't be a masterclass in making a living as an author (that's an entirely different book), it will give you the basics you need to start publishing your series. So, consider this your jumping-off point, one you can use to spark fresh ideas or continue your research elsewhere.

Way back in Chapter One, I said that series are often the best path towards financial success.

In this chapter, it's high time I showed you why.

Packaging Your Series

Once your series is written (or at least underway), you can finally start thinking about all the other pieces that go into a finished novel. Though a solid story is the real core of a successful series, readers *will* judge your books by their covers, often quite literally. Combine that with titling your series, writing blurbs, and creating reader magnets, and you have a bit of work ahead of you to get your series ready to publish.

Of course, all of this works a bit differently for series than for standalones. For a standalone novel, you only have one book to worry about, but a series needs to feel connected on every level—including the packaging.

It's this connection that you really want to pay attention to.

Starting with titles, it's wise to pick a theme that you stick to throughout the series. Pull up your favorite fictional series and read the titles out loud! In all likelihood, they actually *sound* like they go together. They have a similar cadence and rhythm, or follow a consistent format:

- **Patterns:** Where each entry follows the same pattern, phrase, or format. See *Children of Blood and Bone* and *Children of Virtue and Vengeance* from the *Legacy of Orisha* series.
- **Repeat Focus:** Where each entry uses similar imagery or themes. See *The Golden Compass* and *The Subtle Knife* from the *His Dark Materials* series.
- **Character Names:** Where each entry is named for a different character from the series. See *Goose Girl,*

Enna Burning, and *Forest Born* from the *Books of Bayern* series.

- **Connected Events:** Where each entry is named after events from the series. See *The Hunger Games* and *Catching Fire* from *The Hunger Games* series.

This should hold true with your covers as well.

When choosing covers (or hiring a designer), you want to have a consistent visual brand. Your covers should signal the genre you're writing in, but also that these books are related —again, a theme for this section. Flip through any of the novels mentioned throughout this book, and you'll notice they not only sound like a set, but look like one too. This is thanks to consistent color palettes, subject matter, and fonts. Though you don't need each entry to look identical, they should at least look like siblings.

Next, you'll want to consider your blurbs.

These should follow all the best practices you would use for any standalone novel, so I won't cover how to write a book blurb in detail here—I discuss that in depth in *The Ten Day Author* if you aren't sure where to start.

What is different though, is the framing. For a standalone novel, your only concern in your blurb is sharing the story of that book. But for a series, you also need to give context for your reader. Can they jump in at any point of the series, or do they need to start at the very beginning? This is a big potential barrier for readers picking up a new series, so giving them a clear answer (likely at the end of your blurb) can go a long way towards helping their decision.

Last but not least, you'll need a reader magnet.

I'll admit—I was torn on whether to include this in the marketing or packaging section of this chapter. I landed on packaging simply because reader magnets are such a standby of successful publishing that I would never encourage you to publish a novel without one.

But, what is a reader magnet?

Reader magnets are short "bonuses" you offer readers of your series in exchange for their email address, allowing you to stay in touch directly through their inbox. These bonuses can take many forms, from short stories and epilogues, to side quests, dossiers, or even cut content. Typically, you'll promote this in both the front and back of each book you publish, encouraging readers to stay in your orbit.

For series specifically, I recommend writing just one reader magnet that's attractive to readers of the whole series. While you can go beyond that, it involves a lot of extra work, and let's be honest—you're here to write your series, not spend months on your reader magnets. Beyond that though, how to write a *good* reader magnet is a complex topic, one that's been well explored long before this book. If you're serious about building an audience for your series, I recommend both of the *Newsletter Ninja* books by Tammi Labrecque. Those will get you up to speed far better than I can.

Just know that a reader magnet should be on your radar, alongside a healthy email list. Both will serve you well as you build your fan base and get established as a series author.

The Power of Read-Through

With your packaging accounted for, let's talk promotion.

I've said over and over again how series lend themselves to sustainable author careers, but I haven't really justified that claim in full. I've been waiting until this chapter to drop the numbers on you, quite literally—and this is thanks to something called read-through.

Read-through is perhaps the greatest strength of fictional series, and is why they're so attractive to many authors. This is the percentage of readers that pick up books two, three, four, and onwards after reading book one of your series. There's a natural entry point into each subsequent book, meaning (so long as you wrote your series well) readers should be more than happy to stick with you.

To calculate your series read-through, fill in this formula:

Total sales of the last book in the series ÷ Total sales of book one = Series read-through %

Or to calculate the read-through between each individual book, use this formula:

Total sales of book two ÷ Total sales of book one = Individual read-through %

Generally, a series read-through of over 50% is considered healthy, especially when your series is more than three or four books long. If one hundred readers buy book one, your goal is for at least fifty to make it all the way to book eight.

Of course, sometimes that doesn't pan out, in which case that second formula becomes useful. If you're consistently getting a low series read-through, check the read-through between each book to see if there's a sharp drop somewhere in the series. That could be a sign that something about that entry is turning readers away—whether that's negative reviews, a bad cover, or a frustrating cliffhanger.

NOTE: Be careful with your data here! Make sure you're comparing sales for the same period of time across each book, and that you have enough sales to get accurate numbers. If you're new to publishing, you may not have the data for this, and that's ok. Save this formula in your back pocket, and return to it later.

Either way, read-through is the real superpower of fictional series, and it's why series are often sold so differently from standalone novels. Take pricing, for example. Many authors happily discount or even give away the first book in their series, because they know their stories will be enough to pull readers into future entries. Those future sales are where authors make the bulk of their money, which gives readers a lower barrier to entry while still ensuring the author is compensated fairly for their work.

The same goes for marketing.

Rather than having to market and promote six or more books simultaneously, you can focus your efforts on just the first, trusting it'll trigger a knock-on effect as more and more readers enter the series. This lowers the cost of promotions, but more importantly, it also gives you space to breathe.

This all combines to make series an incredibly sustainable option, one that rewards both readers and the authors they love.

Preorders, Pricing, and Promos

With that said, read-through is great and all, but it only works when we ease the transition between books for our readers. When a reader finishes a novel, they're at a crossroad. They're asking themselves a lot of questions, including:

- Is it worth their time to keep reading?
- Do they have the budget to buy that next book?
- Will they enjoy it as much as the last one?
- Could they just wait and come back later (or never)?
- Are they too busy right now?
- Or are there any other books they'd rather read more?

Because of this, hitting that 50% read-through is both about writing an amazing series, but also about reducing resistance. You want to make it easy for readers to brush past these questions and continue through your series, because they know your next novel will be just as good as the last.

There are lots of tricks for doing this, some to do with playing to algorithms (hello, rapid release) and others to do with advertising, targeting, et cetera. Those options are really about keeping your books front of mind as much as possible, basically pinging readers with regular reminders to "hey, buy my next book!"

These tactics are understandably resource intensive, either of time, money, or both. They're great if you can pull them off, but they're also out of reach for many authors. I don't know about you, but I write way too slowly to ever consider something like rapid release!

Luckily, there are other tricks you can lean on to reduce reader resistance, ones that are easy to use at any stage of your career. These serve to smooth the path between books in your series—which is where preorders, back-of-book promotions, box sets, and the always-ubiquitous permafree book come into play.

Preorder Campaigns:

Perhaps the first thing to consider when publishing a series is how fast you'll release each book.

I joked about rapid release a moment ago, but if you're not familiar with that concept, rapid release is where authors publish their novels in incredibly quick succession. This often means launching new books every month or more, with the idea being that readers (and the Amazon algorithm) will take notice, boosting visibility and thus read-through. If you can pull it off, it's a powerful strategy, but it's also an incredibly difficult one.

That's where preorders become useful.

Regardless of how fast you plan to publish your series (within reason), preorders can be a simple way to catch readers at the end of your series before your next entry goes live. You want readers to flow right from book one into book two, without having time to get distracted by other things or overthink their decision. There's a lot competing for our attention these days. Even if a reader loved your novel, it's way too easy for them to forget it exists before the next book comes out.

Preorders make that easy. By offering a preorder for book two right as book one launches, readers are given a natural next step to continue with the series, making it less likely they'll drop off between releases. The danger here is missing your preorder window. Failing to honor a preorder can lead to some serious consequences from retailers, so I don't recommend this option if you aren't confident you can publish the next book before that deadline. However, many platforms allow you to move your preorder date closer if you need to, just not further out.

In this case, you could always set a preorder date far in the future (such as six months away), even if you know your next book will likely go live in just a few months. If anything goes wrong, you have that extra buffer. But if all goes well, you simply adjust the preorder to launch the book "early."

Either way, this is a great way to keep readers hooked on a series, even between releases—and it also provides some comfort that your series will continue in due time.

Back-of-Book Promotions:

Another way authors reduce resistance between books is through back-of-book promotions.

These are the short blurbs or preview chapters often included in the backmatter of novels. When readers finish your book, they're immediately met with an open invitation to start the next one, alongside a call to action linked directly to that book's sales page.

Of course, like anything else, writing these promotions is an art form.

If you plan to include a preview chapter, I recommend limiting it to only the first chapter of the next book. Make sure this opening has a strong hook, and clearly signal that this is the beginning of a new novel—not an epilogue or an additional chapter for the current one. You could even go so far as to include a picture of the next book's cover, to really seal the deal!

Alternatively, you can also write a short two or three-paragraph blurb. Again, your goal is to make buying the next book in your series a no-brainer. What intriguing plot twists, characters, or reveals can you tease? Do you have a fantastic snippet of dialog you could share, or a particular question readers will want answers to?

Whatever will make your next novel tempting to pick up, this is the place for it!

Box Sets:

Box sets are one of those things many authors feel pressured to create, despite the fact that they honestly serve a very niche purpose.

Though shiny and exciting, box sets are generally best saved for late in a series' life. No matter how amazing your series is, it will eventually start to decline. Readers who are interested in the story have largely picked it up, and you've likely moved on to other novels too. In this case, a box set can inject new life into a series, creating renewed interest as well as an easy way for readers to grab the whole set. Typical box sets discount each book by a few dollars, making them an easy "yes" for many people—and thus a low-resistance way to catch latecomers who might otherwise miss your series.

Outside of this though, hang tight on creating a box set.

If your series is new or still selling well, a box set can often cannibalize those sales. Readers will grab the set rather than individual books, and that can starve your series of both sales and visibility.

The exception to this rule is episodic series. Because these series are built around many small installments, episodic authors commonly create box sets whenever a new "season" of the series is complete. In many ways, these stand alone. Some readers simply won't pick up episodic stories until they can binge through a whole season, and some episodic stories are so short that publishing individual entries in print doesn't really make sense. Gathering batches of episodes into larger collections gives you more options for how you market and share your series.

Permafree Books:

Last but not least, let's chat about permafree books.

Permafree books (or permanently discounted books, which are often sold for just $0.99) are novels given away for free, even outside of dedicated promotions. This is incredibly common among series authors because of that read-through we talked about earlier.

Basically, authors want to give readers an easy entry point into their series. They know their series read-through is strong, so they trust most readers will eventually buy the rest of the series, even if they got that first book for free or cheap.

This does *not* mean you need to give away your very first novel, though.

While some authors write prequels or short stories with the express purpose of being a permafree first-in-series, many don't. Instead, much like box sets, this is a strategy you can employ as your series grows. Once you have four, five, or more novels published, it becomes a lot easier to return to that first book, dropping the price once you know your series is established.

If you do so, just keep in mind that your read-through will likely drop sharply between books one and two. This might seem counterintuitive, but the reality is that readers who grab a book for free often never make the time to actually read it—and thus never get sucked into the story. Discounted books definitely have their place, but like all things, it's a strategy you should think about carefully before going all in.

―――――

All of these tactics are really meant to make your series an easy purchase for readers.

Again, there's a natural amount of resistance when buying a book. Readers are wondering if it'll be worth their time, if they'll enjoy the story as much as they think they will, or if they're really in the mood for whatever you're offering. You won't please everyone. But, by easing that transition (and encouraging readers to stay once they've started the series), you greatly increase the chances of your series' success.

My Sample Launch Plan

This is becoming a pretty bulky chapter, but there's one last topic I want to cover—specifically, how you can string this all together into a basic launch plan.

Obviously, we've covered a lot of material, and making sense of it all is often the hardest part. Titling your series, scheduling a discount deal, or adding a back-of-book promo isn't that difficult. But, connecting it into a usable plan often is.

So, let me run you through a quick scenario for how I might approach a six-book series.

First up, I would personally batch at least two or three novels before I started publishing. Thanks to retailer algorithms, our books will start losing visibility after a month or two post-launch. This means I want to publish at a reasonable clip—ideally, once a quarter. Personally, I'm a slow writer, so I know that's the fastest I can manage and that I'll need a buffer to keep myself sane.

With those books ready, book one will go live and book two will be available for preorder. At this stage, I won't stress too much about aggressive promotions. I'll announce the book to my existing audience, but my main focus will be on getting reviews and seeing how the winds blow. How are readers responding? Are my covers attracting the right people? Did my pricing work out? How strong is my blurb, reader magnet, email list, et cetera?

That data will be hugely important as we approach the launch of book two, because it'll help us ensure we're on the right path. It's always possible book one launches to crickets. This can be panic-inducing, but take a deep breath. Often, there's nothing wrong with your story at all. It could be as simple as a bad keyword or a funky title holding readers back, all of which can be fixed. You have this book as a resource, so don't be shy about using it to help with this.

Once book two launches, things can kick into a higher gear.

Book three will go up for preorder right as book two is published, and I'll start pursuing a few more discount deals, newsletter swaps, and other marketing tactics to get eyes on the series. Things aren't at full tilt yet, but we're getting there. We're still collecting data, still pushing for reviews, and starting to plan ahead for book three. We're also doubling down on our back-of-book promos. With book two live, it's easier to see how your read-through is performing, so keep an eye on how well you're guiding readers through the series.

With the launch of book three, it's time to start pulling out all the stops. As before, the preorder for book four will go live alongside book three. I'll drop the price of book one down to $0.99, and I'll run an aggressive week of promotions pointing to that first book. This might seem odd at first, but remember—our goal here is read-through. Even though we have a new book coming out, that's really for our existing readers. While they're picking up book three, we can use that momentum to drive new readers to book one.

This repeats for each subsequent release.

Every time we have another book coming out, the next book goes live for preorder, and we run an aggressive round of promotion to earlier books in the series. Hopefully by now we have a steady readership excited for these stories, meaning we're getting decent visibility and good feedback.

Finally, with the approach of book six, it's time to celebrate!

Personally, I would use this as an excuse to treat my readers to something nice. Perhaps I collect some deleted scenes from earlier drafts to share, or run a live "ask the author" event on Zoom, or even let readers vote on some small part of that final story. They've stuck with us from beginning to end, and I want them to know how much I appreciate them. Combine that with another round of aggressive marketing, and the last book of the series should release on a high note.

With that done, I'd take at least a short hiatus to rest and recover, before looking ahead to the future. Depending on sales, I may consider a box set a year or so down the line, but otherwise I would continue to share and promote the (now complete) series as my readership grows. Though it's no longer my primary focus, there are still plenty of readers who might love that story, and who I'd be happy to welcome into the fan base.

And that's the plan!

Obviously, this is only scratching the surface of everything involved, and it's also just one way to approach this process. There are dozens of creative ways to market and publish a fictional series, but I hope this gives you a better sense of what this could look like in practice. Though it's definitely a lot to juggle, knowing the path ahead is often the first step to making progress.

Lessons from Chapter Thirteen

Publishing a series is an exciting and busy time, but also an overwhelming one.

I do this for a living, and have been coaching and supporting other authors like you for years now. But, despite all that practice, book launches are still exhausting. There's no shame in that, and it's why I encourage you to tackle this in chunks, rather than one huge bite.

I've shared a lot of possibilities in this chapter, but they're really only that—possibilities. You don't need to do all of this at once, and you likely shouldn't. Instead, think of this as a buffet. Pick and choose a handful of techniques that suit your style, and once you're feeling full, give yourself permission to step back and enjoy what you've already done.

You can always return to this in the future if you want to experiment with new options!

In the meantime, here are a few questions to help you apply what you've learned to your story:

- How does the packaging of your series signal to readers that it's a cohesive set?
- Do you have a strong reader magnet pulling readers into your newsletter, and thus your world?
- How will you encourage read-through between each book in your series?
- What will you do to get your first entry in front of new readers?

Once you've answered these questions, I'll see you in our final chapter!

14

KEEPING THE FLAME ALIVE

I t was nine o'clock at night, and I had been sitting at my desk for twelve hours.

I had wrist braces on both hands, shooting pain in my shoulders, and a slowly creeping migraine. But, I couldn't stop—I had a deadline to meet. The next book in my series was due out in a few weeks, and I still had to send it off for formatting, get it to my street team, and a thousand other tiny things that felt like a tall wave about to crash over my head.

I didn't have *time* to rest.

In the end, I did manage to finish that book. Reviews were almost universally positive, and it was the biggest launch I'd had to date. By all accounts it was a rousing success, worth all the sleepless nights I spent racing over the finish line. I wouldn't be surprised if at least a few of my writing students saw that and figured that kind of crunch was supposed to be the norm.

Behind the scenes though, the truth was more complex. Yes, I did get that book published on time. But not before doing serious, lasting harm to my health. It took me months to recover, and in some ways, I'm still feeling the effects even years later. The carpal tunnel that started with that book has never truly gone away, and I look back on that period of my life with a confusing mix of awe and exhaustion.

At the time, I really felt I had no other option.

But in hindsight, most of that pain was self-inflicted.

The idea of "progress" can be an addictive thing, especially once you have a few novels to your name and a small army of readers clamoring for what's next. You want to please them. You want your next book to be better than the rest. You want to keep up with your own expectations.

However, when writing a series, progress isn't always what it seems—and that's why *sustaining* your series is often where the hard work begins. This goes beyond just writer's block, shiny object syndrome, or scheduling, though all of those hurdles are very real. Instead, series present an even deeper challenge, one that I've watched far too many authors (myself included) be consumed by.

Because a series is such a long-running project, it takes a different kind of stamina than most novels. And it also takes a serious look at what progress means to you. So, before our time together comes to an end, here's a heart-to-heart about what it really takes to survive as a series author.

One Thousand Voices

It's a fact of life for authors that we receive an avalanche of "feedback."

There's a lot of noise in this industry, both from other writers as well as from reviewers, beta readers, critique partners, and well-meaning acquaintances. Keeping a thick skin is vital to navigating this storm, but that doesn't mean it won't affect you all the same.

Listen—I don't want to beat around the bush here. Most readers are lovely, but some can be downright cruel. I've received everything from dismissive and sarcastic reviews, to explicit hate mail. It's a frustrating part of being visible in public spaces, and it's something you'll likely experience at least once in your author career.

How do you handle this?

For starters, ignore the haters. They're not your people to begin with. For everything else, though, there's a balance to strike. Some feedback is valuable, but what's unique about being a series author is that your story will probably still be under construction when readers get their hands on it. This means you're still neck-deep in all the planning, writing, and mental work of crafting your series, while also juggling reader feedback.

Both positive and negative feedback can cause trouble here. As an author, you have to know your story and be willing to stay the course even when readers are trying to pull you in other directions. There's a lot to be said for adapting your vision based on what readers enjoy, but there's also a limit to that. If you're constantly being dragged left and right, you'll end up losing the central thread that made your series work so well in the first place.

Fortunately, if you've been following along with this book, you should have a decent sense of the series you're trying to write. Now you just need to find healthy ways to process the noise.

The first thing to consider is who you're talking to.

Not all feedback is created equal, no matter what online trolls try to tell you. Different voices should have different weights, depending on their role in your author career:

- **Editors and Professionals:** The feedback most worth considering. Editors can help you spot and diagnose deep problems in your series in a way few people can.
- **Critique Partners:** As a trusted friend, a good critique partner is a great place to turn for moral support and targeted feedback. Most critique partners are also writers, and can usually point to problems in a story fairly accurately.
- **Beta Readers:** The perfect place for a gut check. The best beta readers are avid fans of your genre, so look for trends in their feedback. Though a single beta comment might not carry much weight, multiple similar comments probably should.
- **Reader Reviews:** The riskiest place to seek feedback. Individual reviews should never be the metric by which you judge your story. Instead, listen for the general consensus, and seek out patterns in the feedback you're receiving. Beware of outliers.

Personally, I strongly recommend seeking support from an editor you trust. When your writing starts to feel like an unending whirlwind of stress, they can step in to help you find solid ground.

I also encourage networking with other authors for the same reason. In such a solitary industry, it's easy to feel like you're the only one struggling when things go wrong. Reaching out to friends in the same space is one of the fastest ways to regain some clarity.

Beyond that though, the type of feedback you seek is largely up to you. Many authors outright refuse to read reviews of their novels, but they're still getting feedback from somewhere. What this looks like for you will be personal, and will likely change as your career unfolds.

When to Pivot Your Series

The second step is deciding what you'll do with what you've learned.

If you're consistently getting feedback that parts of your series are frustrating or disappointing, it may be worth digging deeper to diagnose the problem. Flip back through earlier chapters in this book, consult with an editor, and see if you really need to adjust your original plans.

Sometimes it's ok to stay the course—but in many instances, you may be due for an overhaul.

Facing these revisions can feel shameful, but honestly, this is a natural part of growing as an author. Because series take so long to complete, it's not unusual to write book six while looking back on book one with a tinge of embarrassment. You don't have to feel bad for needing to update your series. It's simply a chance to learn and do better next time.

There are two ways to handle this:

- **Focus on the Future:** With this option, you'll change how you write future books without worrying about past ones. This is a good choice if your series still has a solid foundation, but needs some minor adjustments to address reader concerns.
- **Rewrite and Republish:** If your series needs a major pivot, this might be a good time to redo the entire

set. Unpublish whatever was already released, rewrite the story, and republish it as a fresh series. This is especially helpful if you have lots of bad reviews, though please don't do this unless you actually fix the problems in the original release.

If you didn't write your series all in one go (or if you're expanding the series after writing an initial batch of books), this is a bit easier—but it's still an option for completed series too. Either way, I recommend doubling back to the work we did in Part One and asking yourself:

- What is the overarching concept driving this series?
- What do readers love that I can double down on?
- What trends do I see in the feedback I'm receiving, and how can I address those?
- And what's the soul of this story, the one thing I won't compromise on?

From there, take some time to study. If readers complain that your hero feels hollow, read up on character arcs and archetypes. If they're frustrated with your pacing, grab some books on story structure and plot. Or if your worldbuilding is falling flat, go down rabbit holes on magic systems, technology, and culture.

Here are just a few of the problems you might be facing:

- **Plot:** The story lacks a clear core conflict, leaving the plot without a driving force. To remedy this, get clear on your overarching concept. How is that manifesting in every book you write?
- **Pacing:** The series feels stretched and hollow, or overstuffed. Think carefully about the central thread

of your story. If you have more to say, give yourself space to say it, but otherwise, it may be time to wrap things up.

- **Character:** Characters seem to reset between each book. They change suddenly and unexpectedly, behave inconsistently throughout the series, or sometimes never change at all—even after major events. To avoid this, think about how their experiences will shape them in future books. A series bible can make tracking this much easier.

- **Tone:** Book one is a light and hopeful adventure, while book two is a grizzly psych thriller. Remember that your series makes a promise to readers about the kind of story they're about to experience. Figure out what that promise is, and then keep each entry within a reasonable range. *Jack Reacher* is gritty and intense, while *Nancy Drew* is suspenseful but approachable, and so on.

- **Stakes:** Every entry fully wraps up the story, leaving readers with no reason to continue reading. You do want to resolve the book-specific conflict within each novel, but you should still leave some kind of open loop at the end. What lingering question could you raise, or what hints could you provide about adventures still to come?

All of this really comes down to consistency.

You want to ensure your readers have a positive experience *throughout* your series, and that the promises you made in book one carry through until books ten, eleven, or twelve. This is one of the biggest problems I see with series that otherwise look good on the surface. The author doesn't understand the expectations they've set, and so their series jumps unpredictably between tones, series types, lead characters, and structures.

This is the fastest way to lose otherwise happy readers, because you've betrayed the trust they put into you in that first book. It's also why I keep asking you to return to the overarching concept of your series. If you feel like you've lost that thread, taking time to pause and revise is nothing to be ashamed of.

So long as you hold on to the heart of your story, these "pivoted" books can still feel like a cohesive part of the series— even if they're different from your original vision.

Riding Into the Sunset

Of course, there may come a day when you're truly tired of your series.

Just like needing to pivot, there's no shame here. You're only human! It's perfectly normal to reach a point where you're ready to move on, especially for long-running, expansive series. The key to this is to sunset your series with grace, so neither you nor your readers are left feeling burnt by the whole experience.

First, though, a question:

Why are you itching to move on?

There could be any number of reasons for this, but here are a few common ones to spark some introspection:

- You may be burnt out and ready for a long rest
- You might be called away by new ideas
- A big opportunity might have presented itself, meaning you no longer have space for this series

- Perhaps you're stuck, and the story isn't working the way you intended
- Or maybe sales aren't what you'd hoped for and you know you need a change

Once you know what's spurring this decision, take some time to mourn your series. Yes, really. This was likely a story you were really attached to, and deciding to end it can bring up some strong emotions. Give yourself permission to let go of what "should have happened," and instead take stock of what you have to work with now.

Where are you currently at in the story? What plot threads, character arcs, or subplots do you still need to resolve? Were you building to some bigger conflict, or is this a long-running series that has simply run its course?

Based on that assessment, your number one goal will be to give your series a rousing finale—even if you know you're cutting things short. This will probably require you to write one final book, so think of this as a loving send-off. How you handle this last entry will depend on your series type, but there are some general targets to aim for:

- Try to end on a high note for your plot and cast
- Make sure you've resolved any foreshadowing from earlier books as much as possible
- Show how your protagonist has grown by mirroring the events of book one
- Leave a few mysteries for readers to chew on, but answer the big questions
- Show what life will look like now that the story is over
- And give yourself permission for this final book to be imperfect

For static and anthology series, this process will be slightly different. Rather than stressing about tying off character arcs and conflicts, focus instead on showing *change*. How has your story's world changed since that first entry? How has your cast evolved, how have your readers evolved, and how have you yourself evolved as an author? Aim to give your hero their biggest challenge yet, and then jump ahead, showing how their life has settled down into a new rhythm that brings their story to a close.

Finally, take some time to let go of the story for yourself. There's no use dwelling on it or obsessing over it. So long as you've done your best to give readers the ending they were waiting for, it's ok to cut your original vision short.

Lessons from Chapter Fourteen

In the end, one of the more dangerous parts of writing a series is that readers are always left "waiting."

They're waiting for your next novel to be published. They're waiting to see what happens to that character they love. They're waiting to read about that first kiss, that frightening test, or that trainwreck moment you've been building to since book one.

And quite frankly, that pressure can be difficult to face.

This ends up sucking many series authors into a vicious cycle, one where they push themselves to finish their next book no matter the cost, burning out in the process. Their work isn't as good as it could have been with more time, and they often end up delaying their next release after all. They beat themselves up over their perceived "failure," and may abandon an otherwise amazing series because of it. That level of pressure just isn't sustainable, especially when much of it isn't even real.

This is why, more than any other piece of advice, I want you to put your health first.

Writing a novel is a creative act. It relies on our brain being well rested and inspired, and that means that being productive as a writer isn't the same as other jobs. Staring out the window bored and daydreaming can be productive. Going on long walks can be productive. Anything that gives you space to rest and think deeply about your stories opens the door for your muse to pay a visit.

Even if you aren't planning to sunset your series, it's ok to need a break. If that's the case, say so honestly. Comfort your readers that your series isn't going away (that's often their biggest fear) and be up front that you're taking a short hiatus. Let them know what they can expect in the meantime, perhaps drop a hint or two about all the fun adventures still to come, and then step back. You don't need to promise them anything other than a new novel, and not until you're ready to share it.

I say all of this from experience, but also because there's still part of me that's glued to my desk, struggling to keep up with my own impossible expectations. I'm a perfectionist, and not even a recovering one. This work is deeply fulfilling, but on some days, it's also deeply draining.

No matter what happens in the future, your happiness comes first—and no matter where your series takes you, I hope you deeply love the story you've created. That in and of itself is worth being proud of.

In the meantime, here are a few questions to help you apply what you've learned to your story:

- Whose feedback do you value most as an author?
- What trends are you noticing from beta readers, reviews, and critique partners?
- If you decide to pivot, how much of an overhaul does your series really need?
- How are you prioritizing your health and well-being, even as you keep moving forward?

Once you've answered these questions, this book is complete!

WHAT COMES NEXT?

And, that's a wrap!

Thank you so much for taking this journey through the world of series structure with me. I hope it's given you a lot of clarity around what your future (or current) story might look like, and how you'll gather all the pieces you need to make your series a reality.

As I said at the outset, writing a fictional series is no small feat. Whether you're creating a short, emotional duology or a giant, explosive epic, your story is worth celebrating.

The question now, of course, is where you'll go next.

Honestly, this depends on where you are in the writing process. If you're busy learning about how to craft better novels, I recommend browsing the Further Reading section at the end of this book—and also diving into the rest of The Writer's Craft Series!

At the same time though, I also encourage you to keep writing. I'm a student at heart, so I understand the temptation to hoard as much information as you can. But, eventually, it's time to put that into action. There were tons of prompts sprinkled throughout this book that could serve as a starting point, so consider this your push to put pen to paper.

Last but not least, if you've read and enjoyed this book, it would mean the world to me if you took the time to leave an honest review. As you probably noticed in our chapter on publishing, reviews can make or break a book's success. Even if you only have time to give a star rating, it would do a lot to support this book, and to help other authors decide if it's a good fit for them.

With that said, go out, be creative, and write some awesome series! I'm wishing you all the success in the world.

Happy writing,

Lewis

Before you go... **How well do you really know your hero?**

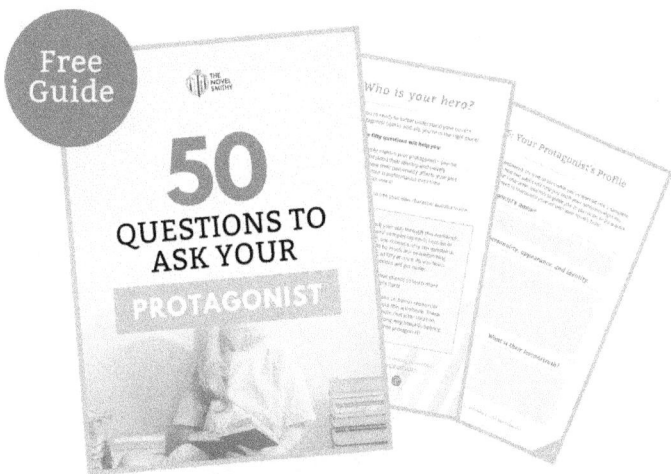

If you're ready to craft a vibrant, engaging protagonist, download your **FREE copy of 50 Questions to Ask Your Protagonist.**

This in-depth questionnaire is the perfect companion to this book, and the perfect way to get to know your hero!

https://thenovelsmithy.com/50-questions/

ABOUT THE AUTHOR

Lewis Jorstad is an editor and book coach who helps scrappy genre fiction authors (and soon-to-be authors) master their craft and find their readers. He's the bestselling author of seven guides for novelists, hosts a thriving community for storytellers inside The Forge, and runs one of The Write Life's 100 Best Websites for Writers.

When he isn't busy supporting students or writing books like this one, he spends far too much time watching squirrels from his office window in Central Virginia.

You can find more of his work over at **The Novel Smithy:**

https://thenovelsmithy.com/

FURTHER READING

I consulted a lot of resources while writing this book, and while developing my own understanding of fictional series over the last few years. While not an exhaustive list, here are a few sources I recommend if you'd like to learn more about either series structure, or the art of publishing and promoting a series:

———

- *Strategic Series Author* — Crystal Hunt
- *Newsletter Ninja* — Tammi Labrecque
- *Newsletter Ninja 2* — Tammi Labrecque
- *Write Your Novel from the Middle* — James Scott Bell
- *Creating Character Arcs* — K.M. Weiland
- *Romancing the Beat* — Gwen Hayes
- *Amazon Decoded* — David Gaughran

ALSO BY LEWIS JORSTAD

THE TEN DAY NOVELIST SERIES

The Ten Day Outline
The Ten Day Draft
The Ten Day Edit
The Ten Day Author

———

THE WRITER'S CRAFT SERIES

Write Your Hero
Mastering Character Arcs
Beyond Book One